I0020370

Availability and Capacity Management in the Cloud

An ITSM narrative account

Availability and Capacity Management in the Cloud

An ITSM narrative account

DANIEL McLEAN

IT Governance Publishing

Every possible effort has been made to ensure that the information contained in this book is accurate at the time of going to press, and the publishers and the author cannot accept responsibility for any errors or omissions, however caused. Any opinions expressed in this book are those of the author, not the publisher. Websites identified are for reference only, not endorsement, and any website visits are at the reader's own risk. No responsibility for loss or damage occasioned to any person acting, or refraining from action, as a result of the material in this publication can be accepted by the publisher or the author.

Apart from any fair dealing for the purposes of research or private study, or criticism or review, as permitted under the Copyright, Designs and Patents Act 1988, this publication may only be reproduced, stored or transmitted, in any form, or by any means, with the prior permission in writing of the publisher or, in the case of reprographic reproduction, in accordance with the terms of licences issued by the Copyright Licensing Agency. Enquiries concerning reproduction outside those terms should be sent to the publishers at the following address:

IT Governance Publishing
IT Governance Limited
Unit 3, Clive Court
Bartholomew's Walk
Cambridgeshire Business Park
Ely
Cambridgeshire
CB7 4EA
United Kingdom

www.itgovernance.co.uk

© Daniel McLean 2014

The author has asserted the rights of the author under the Copyright, Designs and Patents Act, 1988, to be identified as the author of this work.

First published in the United Kingdom in 2014
by IT Governance Publishing
ISBN 978-1-84928-550-6

PREFACE

Companies are continually looking for ways to optimize their provisioning and allocation of resources, such that they can provide essential business services efficiently, consistently and at a justifiable cost. A key service that becomes unavailable can be worse than never having had the service in the first place.

Some organizations consult best practices for the best way to implement availability and capacity management. Best practices are designed to be useful for a large number of companies, in many different environments. Blindly using only best practice recommendations, without adapting them to your particular environment, may leave you at risk. One size does not fit all and definitely not over time. You will need to be thoughtful to ensure what you do is appropriate all the way down to an operational level.

Much of implementing availability and capacity management processes is about changing behavior and mindset. The words in the phrase, *People – Process – Tools*, are in that order for a reason. If people don't embrace the activity, then the Process and Tools won't matter. Changing people's behavior is one of the hardest things we do in business, and something IT people find most difficult.

High performing IT organizations … the ones that succeed … share a common trait ... one that you might not expect to be present in IT organizations. It is this trait that allows them to succeed where others fail.

These organizations learn how to change people's behavior as easily as they change technologies. Changing behavior is one of the most difficult things you will ever do in business. IT is often at a disadvantage because IT organizations are not known for their strong people skills. But that doesn't mean they can't learn.

This is one in a series of books designed to help you understand, at an operational level, how to implement new processes and make the necessary changes to people's behavior.

These fictionalized narratives are based on the actual experience of people just like you ... dealing with the same types of people and issues you face every day.

Look at what worked ... see what failed ... understand the traps to avoid. Learn from the characters' successes and avoid their mistakes.

Please remember that this narrative has been fictionalized. All persons, places, organizations and events appearing in this work are fictitious. Any resemblance to real people, living or dead, is entirely coincidental. Any resemblance to actual places, organizations or events is entirely coincidental.

ABOUT THE AUTHOR

Mr McLean is a consultant who has designed, implemented and operated processes supporting ITSM for over 12 years. He has worked in IT for over 20 years.

He has been involved in the development of global best practice standards and courseware customized to company-specific operational practices and needs. He has worked in the US and the Middle East.

Mr McLean is the author of *The ITSM Iron Triangle: Incidents, Changes and Problems*, *No One of Us Is As Strong As All of Us: Services, Catalogs and Portfolios* and *Integrated Measurement – KPIs and Metrics for ITSM*.

Mr McLean's consultancy focuses on fusing best practices from multiple ITSM relevant standards into practical operational processes, optimized for each organization's particular environment and needs. He provides this support at the design, implementation and daily operation levels.

Among other honors, Mr McLean holds multiple ITSM related best practice and ISO/IEC certificates.

Mr McLean holds both Bachelor's and Master's degrees from Cornell University.

Mr McLean resides in Chicago, Illinois, US.

ACKNOWLEDGEMENTS

I wish to thank the following people, without whom none of this would have been possible.

My clients, users and customers, for allowing me to learn and improve by serving them.

My managers and leaders, for trusting me with opportunities that made me grow.

My peers, for challenging my habits and making me continually assess and improve my deliverables.

My manuscript reviewers: James Ruskin, Network Administrator; IT Governance Ltd and Mart Rovers, President; InterProm USA for their insightful and constructive guidance.

My editors, proofreaders, publishing, marketing and other associates at IT Governance Publishing, for their patience and tireless support, especially Vicki Utting.

My teachers and mentors, for their tolerance of my ignorance, persistence in their instruction, and patience with my endless questions.

My employees, students and mentees, for allowing me to grow by helping them learn.

My family, for tolerating my single-minded focus.

And my wife, Patricia, for being my rock and constant companion.

CONTENTS

INTRODUCTION

IT service management activities can be grouped into two categories; those that focus on processing items related to events or requests, and those that focus on intangible attributes. Availability and capacity are about intangibles.

People often misunderstand the differences between availability and capacity and their roles in ITSM. With the broad acceptance of a variety of Cloud related capabilities, the confusion gets worse. At its simplest level, availability is how long something may be utilized, and capacity is how much of it can be utilized – think of availability as a "yes" or "no" state description of the IT service, while capacity is the "how much" description of the IT service.

Over-zealous marketing of the capabilities of Cloud services often leads people to the incorrect belief that the elasticity and scalability of Clouds virtually eliminates the need for capacity management. Adding Cloud elements adds complexity and requires a combination of business, financial and technical expertise. Don't forget that Clouds are really just tools, and of the trio, People, Process and Tools, the least important item is the tool.

Don't think availability and capacity are less important just because they focus on intangibles. Availability is at the heart of customer satisfaction, but it isn't easy to manage.

Availability management requires an end to end understanding of how any service supports the customer and the infrastructure components required to deliver it. This is very hard for many companies to understand. High-performing incident, problem, change, configuration and service level management are all dependent on a strong availability process.

Capacity management is a proactive assessment of the resources required to meet the demands of the service, both now and into the future. It can have a major impact on your ability to deliver and sustain availability of a service. It creates a more agile IT organization; one that is proactive rather than reactive, and maintains close alignment with the plans and needs of your business partners.

More ITSM initiatives are derailed by the word "service" than any other term you will find. Best practices often talk about service as something that adds value to the business, by helping them achieve their goals. In other words, only the business can define what an IT service is. In too many companies, only IT is involved in defining services.

IT tends to look at services from the inside-out, providing components to the business in IT terms consistent with the way IT is organized. It maximizes the efficiency of IT and minimizes disruptions in IT. The business needs services offered outside-in, end to end packages relevant to specific needs and organized in ways consistent with how the business operates.

High-performing IT organizations understand this. Their goal is to be effective in leveraging business operations, as well as efficient in running their operations. To do this, they must offer views of services that are relevant and understandable to their users, as well as useable within IT.

By itself, this is not an overly complex structure. However, establishing this ITSM process, and maintaining it, depends on something that is highly complex – people's behaviors.

Therein lays the challenge for us all.

CHAPTER 1: ALL TOGETHER NOW

We arrived at the facility on yellow school buses, each of which was segregated by function. Short of a skeleton crew to cover any emergencies, all of IT was here, even the sleepy-eyed third shifters. To the casual observer we must have seemed more like a plague of locusts than a gathering of professionals. Everything had been tightly scripted and scheduled; from fluorescent-vested coordinators with clipboards, to pre-assigned boarding order and seating. Even a military invasion must have involved less planning and management than this soiree.

The trip had been almost silent but it had been clear by the glow of tablets and phones, and the tip-tap of fingers on screens, that the conversation was raucous. The facility had a huge auditorium and was used for all types of civic, cultural and business events. I'd been here before, but never for business reasons. What ticked me off was that this meeting was being held immediately after the close of the business day – on our time, not the company's. If it was so important to the company, why didn't they have the meeting on their time, in the middle of the day?

The sales teams burst off their buses before their buses were even lined up at the entrance to the auditorium. Their teams tried to jostle through the doors, competing to see who would be first into the corporate kick-off of the new sales program ... the one that was going to save what was being rumored as a truly terrible year.

The sales teams clustered in front of the locked lobby doors that led to the auditorium itself, ensuring that when access was finally granted that they would be the first. The other groups – marketing, finance, IT, support, and others, milled about in the lobby but not mixing with each other, much like herds of wild animals wandering across the veldt separately but sharing a common waterhole. No one had planned it that way; it just seemed to be the natural inclination of everyone there.

While some of the groups talked and the service desk members even raised some noise, I was not surprised that the IT teams fell into the stereotype they had shown on the bus and stood silently, messaging each other electronically. It always felt somewhat creepy to be standing amongst a group of people who were interacting at a ferocious pace but the only sound was the tapping of fingers against screens, framed by an occasional giggle.

Food had been placed on tables scattered through the lobby. Probably an attempt by leadership to make sure there wasn't a riot. Putting food in front of a group of IT people was like offering food to a swarm of locusts. Drop it off and get away quickly, before you lose any fingers. By the time I fought my way to the table, there wasn't much beyond packets of condiments and a few napkins scattered around. Talking to others, I discovered our leadership had provided us with steamed hot dogs, chips, brownies and chocolate chip cookies, all washed down with sugary soft drinks. Knowing that, I felt better I'd missed the food.

Finally, the coordinators in orange security vests, with their clipboards at the ready, herded us into the auditorium, one functional group at a time. It seemed attendance was being taken. I looked closely at the burly monitor checking our team off on his list. I'd never seem him before and he was not someone you would easily forget. He wasn't wearing a company badge and wouldn't have looked out of place as a bouncer at a biker's bar on dollar beer night.

I stifled a laugh when Mukasa, one of the application developers walking behind me, broke the electronic curtain of silence and actually spoke. With a pronounced Midlands-inflected accent, he said, "You'd think they were worried the IT folks were going to riot and they needed to bring in the SWAT team just in case we unleashed some rogue software loose on them."

Finally, we made it into the main auditorium. More orange-vested coordinators directed us to our section. We were grouped by function, with small spaces left between each group, lending credence to Mukasa's idea that the coordinators were more accustomed to handling drunks ready to fight, than teams of professionals here for a leadership command performance.

The lights in the seating area were off, but the reflections from the spotlights and lasers swirling on the stage cast a glow bright enough for me to follow the person in front of me to my seat. The experience was overwhelming. The stage had a curtained backdrop that twinkled under the dance of lights and theatre smoke rising from the stage. Hanging in front of the curtain were six enormous monitors, each playing video pictures of the company, cross-cut with vignettes of the executives and their families. There was no sound from the individual screens. Instead, there was the gut-shaking thump of a beat-heavy trance club mix swirling around the room.

The IT people sat silently in the glow of their electronic devices, while the marketing teams were gyrating to the music. Someone in the support group had acquired a large plastic ball they were bouncing overhead, being ever so careful not to let it stray into the airspace of another group.

While most of the people were occupied in their own version of killing time, senior managers were standing at their seats, oblivious to the environment around them. Some were gesturing with their fingers and others taking notes. As near as I could see, they were counting heads for their teams. An open hand slapped lightly against my back. I turned as Sean gestured toward the counters and said, "Good thing you made it. Would hate to see you removed from the company for a dumb mistake. Make sure you are seen by your manager, so your attendance is duly noted."

"It's voluntary, last I checked."

Sean laughed. "Sorry, I didn't notice your yellow pigtails, perky smile and your cute little dog." He whistled loudly, then shouted out his manager's name. When his manager turned to look, Sean waved and yelled, "Please mark me present, sir." His manager grimaced and nodded back at Sean, then continued his counting.

Sean had been with the company for a long time. When he'd started, it was a young company with a small cluster of people in IT. He knew all of the original executives personally, because he'd worked with them. He'd seen a lot of people come and go. He'd been here so long, I was half convinced that he'd been born in a conference room. His fingerprints were all over almost every system and tool IT had ever built or installed. I'd met him the first week I came onboard, and he always seemed to know the answer to any question I could ask. More importantly, he always took the time to answer any question I put to him.

1: All Together Now

I liked working with Sean because he knew so much about the way this organization operated, and about all those things people never write down. You just had to wade through his sarcastic manner of dealing with people and the frustrating realization that, because of his longevity and personal relationships with senior leaders, he could get away with behaviors that would have anyone else fired in a heartbeat.

Laughing, Sean threw himself down into the seat beside me. "Since when has anything you've ever been asked to do here been anything but a command performance"?

In the nine months I'd been here, I'd learned that Sean was generally correct when it came to matters about the company. He was right about this event.

This was a command performance to launch a new application called CET, the Customer Engagement Tool; an application to support a major improvement of the company's customer relationship management capabilities.

Leadership was promising CET was the savior of what, up until now, had been eight months of dismal sales results. The implicit message to IT was that if this new tool didn't fix that revenue problem, there would be less money and fewer people in IT next year.

I'd seen this approach used at quite a few companies to motivate the sales teams. It was the kind of thing that energized people with their mindset.

It was the equivalent of one size fits all. What had never made sense to me was how leadership always seemed to think things which motivated sales teams would also motivate IT people, such as developers – creators who had a reputation for being arrogant, moody and disagreeable, with a fondness for shooting down ideas and endlessly debating pedantic details. These were often people who last saw sunlight three months ago and subsisted on a diet of coffee, Chinese food, and anything that you could put hot sauce on. The message might be transferable, but it always seemed to me that the form of the message should have been tuned to the intended audience.

However, someone in senior leadership had decided it was better to use an afternoon of our personal time and the company's money, rather than promoting products, or buying new tools, or hiring needed employees. So I trusted they knew what was best, and in this case, it was to spend all of these resources on a circus.

The room darkened, and people quickly took their seats. Conversation dropped to a minimum. Just before it went completely dark, the entire room exploded in sight and sound. Strobing laser lights danced out from the stage and across the attendees ... jerking in time to pounding house music, loud enough to make the floor rumble like there was an earthquake. The monitors on stage flashed to white-out, then faded to a rapid-fire mélange of company buildings, people, and products. Each screen showed a different set of pictures. Slowly, the screen images synchronized on an image of Jonah, our CEO, grinning at the audience from each screen. As he opened his mouth, all of the music stopped and the room was strangely quiet. You could almost hear people breathing.

"Welcome to our kick-off of CET," bellowed his image. On the screen, graphics of charts and graphs appeared behind him, all showing inexorable growth from the rollout of CET. "Our kick-off unites us company-wide. From those here in the building, to those around the world viewing us live, we are all one team; one team focused on a single goal ... one team exploding into new heights of sales and profits ... one team setting new records again this year – but only if you want it hard enough. Do you want it? Let me hear you. Do you want it"?

The audience erupted into screams and cheers. People jumped to their feet and began clapping ... chanting Jonah's name.

With an explosive rumble, each image of Jonah turned and gestured, as if pointing to the rear of the stage. Out from behind the curtain ran Jonah, dressed just as he was in the video. The monitors instantly switched from recorded to live feed. Visible on all monitors simultaneously, Jonah ran back and forth across the edge of the stage. Wireless mini-mike on the side of his head, he pointed at the cheering crowd, calling out people's names and teams.

"Are you ready for success"? he yelled, never slowing for a moment. "Are we the best? Are we the winners? Are we the ones our customer's need"?

People screamed with each question, and that only seemed to pump him up even more.

"Then let's meet the rest of our leadership team. The people who will guide us all into the future."

From alternating sides of the stage, the senior leadership team ran onto the stage, one at a time, as Jonah called their names, while a video montage of them around the company played on each of the monitors. One by one they gathered behind him, slapping backs and shaking hands, as strobes pulsed and music boomed. As the last ran onto the stage and joined the others, the music reached its peak, the monitors went pure white, and the room lit up completely bright with every light on full. The lights blinked like a giant flashbulb and settled back to normal, with the entire senior leadership team sitting in chairs arranged in a semi-circle, with Jonah standing in the center at the edge of the stage.

The people in the auditorium jumped to their feet and erupted into applause. Jonah waved everyone to be quiet and sit down. After a few moments, the room settled into silence.

"Thank you ... thank you all for taking the time out of your valuable day to be here," said Jonah. "But we are not alone. We are united around the globe. Through the expertise of our world-class IT team, every member of our organization is now part of this meeting ... united as one ... unified in our drive to make CET a success."

Jonah spun and pointed at the monitor over his left shoulder and shouted, "Give me Helsinki." The picture shifted to an auditorium, not unlike this one, filled with wildly cheering people. Jonah spun around and pointed to the screen over his right shoulder and yelled, "Give me Mumbai," and it filled with yelling people. Jonah pointed to a third monitor and shouted, "Give me Tokyo." Another screen full of screaming people appeared.

Jonah ran to the edge of the stage and yelled, "Now for the star of this show ... CET."

The screens switched instantly to the familiar opening interface of CET. Attendants ran out from the wings and passed out tablets and laptops to the leadership sitting on stage.

1: All Together Now

Jonah pointed to the monitors where each senior leader could be seen logging into CET. "This is to show that your leadership team has no problem getting its hands dirty."

Laughter rang through the auditorium.

At each site, other leaders began logging into CET. The screens filled with data and the various inputs of CET. It was an amazing piece of design and coding, and it looked beautiful.

But only for an instant.

Without warning, the picture on one of the on-stage monitors lost sync, turned to static, popped off and the screen faded to black. An instant later, two other screens went dark ... followed one at a time by every other monitor on stage. Although we couldn't see their screens, it was immediately apparent that the leaders were having the same response on their machines. Attendants ran out from the wings of the stage and worked feverishly trying to get them working, but with no success.

The room went silent for a moment before IT phones started lighting up. Network managers and engineers ran from their seats towards the lobby, while others started working their tablets with great purpose.

Jonah stood near the edge of the stage. With a forced smile, he said, "This goes to show you that no plan ... however great, ever survives contact with reality ... regardless of how world-class your IT department may be. Stuff happens, and we must be prepared to ..."

With a loud pop, all of the wireless microphones went dead. Whilst we could see Jonah's lips moving, no one could hear a thing.

Sean leaned over and whispered, "Rule number one of corporate survival. Never, ever, embarrass the CEO and the rest of the executive leadership team in public. I smell some firings in IT coming, just as a warning not to let this happen again. If I were you, I'd keep my head down."

Fortunately, the monitors flickered back to life after a few minutes and sound returned to the microphones shortly thereafter. The leadership team resumed where they had left off; showing us how CET was better than anything the competition had, and was a response to many customer complaints and suggestions.

Jonah and the leadership team did their best to whip the audience excitement back up, but the moment seemed to have been lost. They covered everything they'd set out to share, but while the content was there, the emotion had been drained from the room. You want your new world-beating service to be invulnerable, the juggernaut we needed to succeed. CET had shown us it was vulnerable before it was even fully launched. The worst part was we didn't know what it was vulnerable to. All I knew, and all everyone there knew, was that it could fail without a lot of effort.

It was a solemn group that filed out of the auditorium and onto the buses. It was the antithesis of the group that had gone in. Rather than surging out ready to take on the world, we looked like a long line of prisoners ... beaten down people with no hope, who were just mindlessly going through the motions. If the purpose of the meeting had been to whip up our fervor, the meeting had been a failure. In fact, it had left us worse off than when we started.

Sean walked beside me. "Notice what's missing"?

1: All Together Now

I shook my head.

"All those engineers who ran out to respond to the disruption. That probably means they are still trying to figure it out. That's bad, because the longer it takes IT to come up with an answer, the more bodies leadership will want. It's bad enough to embarrass them in front of the entire company, but to then not be able to immediately tell them why ... with absolute certainty ... then people will be made to publicly suffer, as a warning for the next time."

"Well, at least this time it doesn't impact me," I snapped back.

The ride back on the IT bus wasn't much different from the ride out ... rows of techies fingering their technology toys. Not me. I sat there hoping IT wasn't going to get beat-up for embarrassing the CEO in front of the entire company. After all, stuff breaks, regardless of how well you build it. And things always break at the most inconvenient time. Everyone in business understood that, didn't they? At least I could feel comfortable knowing that there was no way this could be tagged to me.

That thought had just cleared my head when Ricardo, my manager, walked down the aisle and stood beside me. He was talking on the phone. "That sounds right, Jessica. We'll talk in the morning."

Jessica was our CIO.

Ricardo leaned over and said, "Chris, there will be a meeting in my office tomorrow morning. Please be there. My admin will send you the time."

I nodded, "No problem," but hoped as hard as I could that Jessica wasn't planning to be there.

Tips that would have helped Chris

1. Expand your perspective. Everything you work on for customers will be easier, and more useful, if you are exposed to how other groups within the company, its activities, and its goals, are presented to those customers. Never pass up a chance to see how others outside IT work and what they do.
2. IT's impact ranges far beyond traditional support in areas such as accounting. There is little done in the corporation that isn't dependent on the proper functioning of IT. Untoward events can have impacts way beyond what you expect, and bring the entire company to its knees.
3. Many people confuse availability and capacity. This is especially common for people who don't deal with it on a regular basis, or are removed from it by their role in the organization. You must be an evangelist, constantly spreading the word, and telling people what the difference is and why it is important.

CHAPTER 2: ONE BIG, HAPPY FAMILY

I sat in Ricardo's office, waiting for him to arrive. He was late. Deidra, his administrative assistant, told me he'd had a breakfast meeting with Jessica, our CIO. Assuming Jessica hadn't simply fired him on the spot, as the first sacrificial victim, he was probably getting some very ugly, detailed, and direct feedback about yesterday's event, and what was expected of him going forward. I tried to convince myself that I had nothing to worry about. It was his other teams that were involved, not me.

I'd been reporting to Ricardo for the last few months. He hadn't had a lot of experience in our industry, but his children attended the same day school as those of Jessica. After his start-up company had gone out of business, she'd made an extra special effort recruiting him to come to work here. He knew nothing of our business when he arrived, and my job for the first month seemed to consist of educating him, since Jessica didn't have the time to do it.

There had been nothing formal from Jessica, and no new goals added to my plan. That all meant I'd get no credit for any of the work, and still be responsible for my existing goals. It was the typical task where leadership assumed you could always do more, if you would only work as hard as they did, and from what they could see, no one in the company worked as hard as they did. That's one of the reasons they felt justified with their incredible compensation packages ... that, and they felt they had to make all the "hard" decisions.

At first, I really resented that I had been given the responsibility for training my leader, because his leader, our

CIO, had hired someone for a critical position who didn't have the slightest idea of what we did, or how to do it. The idea that I was training my boss on the fundamentals of his job really bothered me. If he was so worth bringing on board that our CIO had personally recruited him, shouldn't he have at least known something about his job?

It wasn't like I was a translator for someone who didn't speak the language. He seemed smart, but totally clueless about what we did and what was important. She could just as well have picked someone fresh out of school with no work experience. Part of me toyed with the idea of teaching him things that would make my life much easier, like I could work from home every Friday and Monday – but I couldn't do that ... it wouldn't be right ... it wouldn't be ... fair. And strange as that word sounded here at work, I wasn't going to stoop to giving up my standards of what was right and wrong just to get ahead.

I was surprised when Ricardo quick-walked into the office full of smiles and gave me a happy, "Good Morning. Sorry I am late. Jessica and I have children in the same school and we were talking about being chaperones for the school's field trip next week, and we lost track of time. When you have kids, it's easy to lose time. Do you have any children, Chris"?

I shook my head. "No." He seemed exceedingly perky for a man who should have just received a thorough beat-down by his boss.

"You ought to settle down and find the time. They're a lot of work, but C ...," Ricardo paused, smiled, and said, "And they give you something in common with so many people. That can be a real advantage in business as a conversation starter."

I nodded and said, "Thanks," as he motioned me into his office.

I went to shut the door behind me, but he stopped me, "Leave it open. We'll be heading out in a moment. We're just waiting for a couple of other people."

I nodded, but still couldn't figure out that if the issue was with the application, what all the developers and testers had been doing these last six months. More importantly, had anyone in possession of detailed facts concluded it was the app's problem, or was that just leadership exercising their opinion?

Did my opinion even matter?

I got ready to take notes. I didn't care why I was here; I just hoped I could keep my portion of work down to a minimum. I needed to keep my regular job moving along. I already had to educate Ricardo on how things worked here, in addition to all my other work, so there wasn't much time for disruptions. Somehow leadership always seemed to assume that special projects could be done while still getting the rest of one's work done, as if they haven't assigned us enough work, and we're just hanging around drinking coffee all day.

"Obviously, it's embarrassing that IT failed executive leadership and the rest of the company. But it's history, and we can't go back and change our missteps. Fortunately, our executive leadership anticipated this eventuality, and had arrived at an approach to give us the flexibility going forward."

I wrote down the phrase, "More testing using contract testers," in my notebook.

"Jessica, legal, and some of the senior leaders from the business have been working with this company for the last two months. I've got a lot of experience reinforcing company capabilities using augmentation. It's one of the reasons she brought me onboard. This company will help us ensure success. We need everyone's help to ensure CET has the capability to support the needs of the business. So you need to put aside any prior company cultural concerns and embrace the new solution. Since you haven't been here as long as most, it should not be a problem. We all must evolve."

Ricardo leaned across the desk towards me and in a quiet, but very firm voice, said, "I know from experience that when we use augmented resources it is important to have someone manage those external resources from our company's perspective. No one seems to have the breadth of knowledge of the company and flexibility to adapt to this new role. That is why I am assigning this role to you. You will be our liaison to the operational activity of this company."

"Augment"? I asked. I knew what the phrase meant, but I couldn't believe what he was saying. "And you want me to be the owner of this? Why"?

Ricardo gave me a rather annoyed look, much like one might give an obstinate child. "Augmenting our capabilities allows us to provide from the most appropriate and capable source for the situation. You know, like augmenting an organization's staff to deal with non-core issues, so as to free employees to focus on their area of specialty."

"That's a huge change in direction for us as a company. I know you haven't been here a long time, so you may not have an appreciation for how hard the company works to do everything itself. After all, no one can give you as well-matched a solution as you can develop in-house. That's why we built CET in-house, and plan to operate it from here."

Ricardo pushed himself a little away from the desk. Slowly, he crossed his legs, then carefully adjusted the pleat on his pants and picked a few pieces of lint off the material. Leaning back in his chair, he interlocked the fingers of both hands and placed them against his chest.

He sat staring at me for a moment before speaking.

"Chris, we have only known each other for a little while, but I think that we have made great strides in building a good relationship based on trust and a mutual commitment to the success of the company. Initially, I had the same caution about this type of change as you do. However, these decisions are based on evaluations conducted by our leaders. In the time I have been here, I have come to know many of our senior leaders well, and I must tell you that I respect their vision as the right vision for the company."

Ricardo leaned forward slightly. "And in the end it will be what it will be, and it is up to each of us, individually, to make it work for the good of all. That's why we are right-sourcing the operationalization of CET."

"Call it like it is," I blurted. "You're talking about outsourcing. But we do everything in-house. We even build and run our own websites," I protested. I didn't mention that our social media program was ten years out of date. But up till now, no one had dared consider outsourcing any of it. That would mean a reduction in work, and potentially a loss of technical jobs.

"You're being inflammatory in your words, Chris. They are what I would call escalating words. What we need to use now are analytical words ... words based on facts, without a lot of emotional baggage."

I sighed. "I don't mean to be disrespectful, but have you been here long enough to have conducted an evaluation necessary to make that kind of recommendation? Isn't there some middle ground we should consider? Perhaps they would be open to a compromise"?

Ricardo shook his head slightly. "What leadership has decided is what is right for the company. That is what matters. Compromise on these types of issues will merely muddy the waters for you and me, and everyone else."

That was one of the things I hated about Ricardo. Everything seemed right or wrong to him. There was never room for compromise or negotiation. Even when he asked for your input, it seemed like he had already made his decision and was just trying to see which side you were on.

When he'd first arrived, I'd made the ignorant assumption that, by his accent, name and slightly different way of approaching business situations that he'd grown up, and had been working in South America before he came here. I was expecting someone with a different cultural spin on their work than most of the people here, but Sean told me that was nonsense. Not only had Ricardo been born and raised in Oklahoma City in the US, but his parents and grandparents had also been born and raised there. In fact, Sean had been told by a friend in HR that Ricardo didn't even have a passport. He'd never even been out of the country. All of the South American businessman and their ways of doing business was nothing but an affectation. I didn't know why, and it didn't really matter, other than it told me he felt some kind of weakness that he felt he could offset by pretending to be someone he was not.

Halfway through my thought, I heard a knock behind me, then Ricardo said, "Glad you made it okay. Come on in. How was your flight"?

"On time and quiet for a change. The nice thing about morning flights is fewer tourists and screaming babies. I do my best to separate myself from them, so I can be productive during the flight, but you wouldn't believe how many ignorant parents waste first class tickets on their screaming offspring."

That voice sounded so familiar. I just couldn't place it.

"Flying can be stressful for everyone," said Ricardo. "And I believe you already know, Chris. Chris will be our contact point for this project."

"Oh, yes. Chris and I go back a long way. We have quite a bit of history together, don't we Chris"?

I turned around in my chair, and was unable to hide my surprise.

It was Lee. Not that long ago I had worked for him, and he nearly had me fired just to demonstrate to his peers how tough he was. Fortunately, I escaped simply with an impossible performance improvement plan, after which he lost interest in me and left with a promotion to run an entire field division before I could be terminated.

He was impossible to miss. From his tall, flawless patrician features, to perfectly coiffed hair, an immaculate Brioni suit showing no wrinkle or crease or any other evidence of having been stuffed in an airplane, a Patek Philippe watch ticking silently on his wrist, and a shining pair of Gaziano

& Girling shoes. No one I had ever seen in business was so invested in their appearance. But that was Lee, just as I remembered him, all surface and no substance.

"Hi, Lee. I thought you were running a division for us"? I said, forcing a smile as I extended my hand.

"You need to stay informed, Chris," He gave a sigh of disappointment. "I know I tried to teach you that." He gave me a minimalist two-pump handshake and let out a theatrical sigh through a small smile. "After I restored some order there, I needed new challenges and this new company seemed just made to order."

Standing slightly behind Lee was a short, much rounder man, with stacks of binders and papers under his arms. He was the antithesis of Lee. He wore rumpled and wrinkled clothes, with an old stain on his shirt and glasses so dirty I could see the fingerprints from where I sat. He was flushed, breathing hard and sweating. He gave every appearance of having flown here this morning in the baggage hold, sandwiched between several occupied caskets and a female Rottweiler in heat. He looked up at Lee, waited for a response, and then stuck his hand out in my direction. "Hi. I'm Sherm. I guess we'll be working together on this project."

Lee gestured to Ricardo and said, "And I believe you met my associate, Sherman, during our last visit," he sniffed.

"Of course," said Ricardo. "How are you Sherman"?

"Sherm, just call me Sherm, please," he said. As he released my hand, I realized it was now a little sticky from something that smelled like orange marmalade.

2: One Big, Happy Family

Lee slowly pulled out a leather-bound folio and removed a fountain pen from his inside jacket pocket. We all sat silently as he unscrewed the top and then adjusted his position in the chair. Sherm kept looking nervously back and forth between the pile of documents he'd carried in for Lee. Sherm started to speak and Lee held up his hand, a single finger extended in the air, and he fell silent.

I'd seen this before. He'd done it to me all the time. It was his way of controlling the conversation. I hated it but still admired how Lee could so effortlessly make himself the focal point of any meeting.

Finally, settled, Lee looked up and staring directly at me said, "So tell me, Chris ... by the way, I really enjoyed having you working for me on my team. Your leadership has indicated there is a capacity problem related to a critical new application, and they've contracted with my company to provide flexible, burstable supported capacity for this new application, as well as first-level support. In other words, they want us to host it using our advanced Cloud capabilities, to avoid debacles like the kind that happened yesterday. So I'd like to confirm a few things, if you don't mind. Please tell me, specifically, about your capacity management process, procedures, participants, meetings, and activities ... things like that. We have our own methods, but as you know, I am always open to learning and gaining insight from others."

My brain stumbled and stuttered at such a bold lie. I'd never seen Lee interested in anyone else's opinion other than his own, and to never do anything without already knowing the answer and what he planned to do. I managed to choke out, "I don't know if we have anything relevant. I have very little knowledge ..."

Lee cut me off and made a quick note. He nodded and said, "That's what we were led to believe."

"It's not my area of responsibility," I protested. "We may have something. It's just that I am not aware ..."

"No need to be defensive, Chris." smiled Lee. "The first step to improving is to know what you're not doing and understanding your personal limitations."

I looked to Ricardo, but he was nodding as Lee talked. It looked like Lee had won another convert, and without even speaking to him. I was afraid Lee was back here to finish the job he'd started, to get me fired. This was not going to end well for me. I knew it.

Tips that would have helped Chris

1. Leaders often fail to look at opportunity costs, or lost costs, when it comes to your participation in activities important to them. The approach of over-including people provides safety and protection, by ensuring no one is left out. Unfortunately, while your presence provides them with that coverage, your deliverables do not change. In other words, you must still meet your deadlines, so effectively you are reducing risk to leaders concerns by increasing the risk for your deliverables to them. Try to consider the impact these events have on you and provide the tradeoffs as alternatives to leadership, to ensure they consider all the issues in their decisions.

2. Words, speech, documents, and other forms of communication, are out of your control once you send them out. Although you may try to restrict who receives them, in the end they will travel anywhere and everywhere. More importantly, they will need to stand on their own without further comment or context from you. Be thoughtful about what you say of others, as it may come back to haunt you.

3. In times of crisis ... real, or manufactured, or imaginary, it is essential to stick to the facts. Speculation has no place there. This is especially true when speaking with leadership. Generally, they will lack your depth of subject matter expertise and will have a number of other ongoing pressing issues. They will not hear your qualifiers and instead only hear the speculation as fact.

CHAPTER 3: WHO WANTS TO SUPPORT THIS SERVICE?

The first meeting of the capacity planning team was not quite as easy, or simple, as we had hoped.

I arrived at the conference room almost ten minutes early. Showing up before everyone else was one of my compulsions. I hated being late for meetings almost as much as I hated people being late for mine. It was such a show of disrespect, as if the time of all the others at the meeting was collectively less important than yours. That was especially true for important meetings, and from all the signs, this one was definitely going to be important. Besides, it gave me a few minutes alone with my thoughts so I could review what I expected to accomplish.

The conference room was dominated by a long, rectangular table. Its cheap vinyl finish was scored and scarred from years of abuse. A tangle of twisted wires from a mismatched brace of speaker phones disappeared down a hole in the center of the table. At the far end of the room, an enormous white board, stretching from ceiling to floor, hung on the wall. The faded ghosts of not quite erased lettering and lines echoed its surface, showing where some misguided presenter had used a permanent marker to make their point. Judging by the stains on the carpet, the marks on the wall, and the hand prints on the table, the room hadn't been cleaned in a long time.

I carefully selected my seat and wondered how many people were going to attend. This was a big conference room with over a dozen chairs, in various states of repair, clustered around the table.

I'd been sitting quietly, alone with my thoughts for about five minutes, when the door opened and Sean walked in. He was invaluable to work with because he knew so much about all those things people never write down. His encyclopedic knowledge and confidence allowed him to intimidate some people, or diffuse almost any crisis.

"I love your new office," joked Sean with a smile, just before he dropped his tablet down onto the table and threw himself into one of the old chairs. It was so wobbly that for a moment I thought it would fall over, but somehow he kept it upright.

"What's this about"? I asked innocently. I knew Lee and Sherm would be here. I just wanted to see if Sean had already found out about it.

"I heard we're going to have consultants today," said Sean with a laugh. "You know, people who know nothing about our business but somehow have a magic power that allows them to instantly understand what needs to be addressed and how to fix it. I'm impressed already and they're not even here yet."

Without warning, Jessica walked into the conference room. She was in the company of Lee, my former manager. I was shocked at first, but then realized that if she and the rest of the leadership had been working with him and his company for several months, it only made sense she knew him.

This company was like most of the others I'd worked for. Putting someone on a performance improvement plan, such as Lee had done to me, wasn't really intended to rehabilitate an employee or teach them how to become, and align, with the company's values, despite all the official wording and process surrounding it. PIPs were put in place as an informal notification that you were no longer wanted around here, and to provide the appropriate documentation for your soon to be departure. Ideally, that would be voluntary, but if you were too dim to recognize the request, or too stubborn to acquiesce, it would turn from a resignation to a firing by the end of the PIP.

Lee had put me on an impossible performance improvement plan to get me fired, as a demonstration of his power. It had nothing to do with my work. The only thing that saved me was he wangled a promotion for himself to run an entire division for the company. I didn't understand why he was back here.

Lee sat himself down regally at the head of the conference room table, talking with Jessica as she took the seat to his right. It was as if he'd never left.

"After I finished rebuilding that field division here, I decided I needed some new challenges. I had completed most of what I wanted to accomplish here, so I resigned and moved on to a new company, heading up sales and marketing. I took a little time off between jobs before heading up sales and marketing for my new company. I went to visit my brother and his family in Singapore. He's there on assignment for his company. They're living in the Tanglin Village neighborhood – near the botanical gardens. Very nice area. You're very cosmopolitan. You must have been in Asia before, perhaps you've been to Singapore and are familiar with the area," said Lee, as he leaned forward toward Jessica and smiled.

Jessica smiled back and shook her head.

"I'm sure that you would love it … such a clean and orderly city. My brother and his wife wanted their children to have the benefit of the international experience but in a bilingual environment, so the children would not be handicapped when they eventually returned to the US. They managed to get them into the Chinese International School on Dunearn Road. It really appealed to them because it offered an accredited English-Mandarin education program. It's very small, so there is a lot of personal attention, but it is also extremely selective about admissions. Fortunately, the managing director of the company my brother works for has some contacts at the school, and managed to get the children into the program. After all, why should successful and essential people like us be distracted from our larger mission by waiting in line with everyone else"?

Jessica sat, raptly staring at Lee ... drawn in by his stories and the way he seemed to find a way to relate to anyone, even if they had initially seemed to have nothing in common. He was good, there was no doubt about that ... much better than I could ever be, and I think I might have even hated him a little more for that than for the fact that he once tried to have me fired, just to show he could.

Sherm stumbled into the room, his arms clutched around a pile of papers, with a laptop over one shoulder and a portable projector over the other. "Sorry I'm late. I got lost."

Lee looked up. He checked the ostentatious gold watch on his wrist and made a slightly annoyed face. "Perhaps you should get set up and begin."

Sherm unpacked the projector and hooked it to the laptop. Just as he finished, Sean leaned across the table and handed him the video connector for the large monitor on the wall at the head of the room. In a quiet voice, Sean said, "You might want to use this instead. It will give you a better picture."

Sherm looked at the cable and then the projector sitting on the table, then rolled his eyes and shook his head. As he reconfigured the equipment, Lee pulled out a business card and wrote on the back of it before passing it to Jessica. "I'm staying at this hotel for the next few weeks until everything is working to your satisfaction. Call me anytime if you have any concerns. Perhaps we can have dinner some evening, so you can give me some extended feedback and we can catch up some more."

Jessica nodded. "Of course, I'd love that."

Yes, I decided. I still really hated Lee.

Sherm finished connecting the equipment and passed out documents to everyone in the room. When he was finished, he stood quietly at the head of the room, staring at Lee.

After visually surveying what Sherm had done, Lee said. "Why don't you begin, Sherman?" He stopped for a moment, turned to Jessica, extended his hand toward her and said, "With your permission, of course."

Jessica smiled and nodded. "Please continue, Sherman."

Sherm hit a button on the laptop and a moment later a promo video of their company streamed onto the screen, complete with their CEO talking about her organization's team and their capabilities. The problem was that this was information much more appropriate to a pre-sales meeting and not a kick-off of the operational process. That meant that in his enthusiasm and excitement, Sherm was missing something very important – he was losing his audience. All around me people were drifting off into other things. Some were skimming through the handout. Others were discreetly sending out text messages, or quick scanning e-mails via their phone.

Sean leaned over and whispered to me, "If Jessica weren't here, people would be bailing out, especially the business representatives. But that will only help for so long. Being enthusiastic is good, but it doesn't help very much if no one is interested in what you're talking about. Didn't anyone ever tell him to stop selling once the deal is signed? I guess that's why pre-sales and post-sales teams always seem to be different people."

Finally, Lee stood up and motioned for Sherm to stop the presentation. "Thank you very much, Sherman. I think I can handle things from here." Lee walked to the front of the room. Sherm sat down near him, taking the laptop, so he could run any necessary presentations.

"First, let me thank each of you, and your senior leadership, for the trust they have placed in us by allowing us to help you continue your history of continual, profitable growth. We have a long history of success in helping companies achieve their goals. And through our advanced and flexible technology, we will continue to help them and you."

Lee gestured to Sherm and said, "Analysis slides, please."

A series of charts appeared on the screen. Lee pointed to a series of green and blue lines snaking across the bottom.

"This is data we collected on your company several months ago, when we first began discussions with your leadership."

He pointed to an orange line running straight across the middle.

"This represents your utilization capacity for various applications. Today, you can process no more than this amount of application activity. If you do, events like the one you experienced during the kick-off will become commonplace, and there will be no easy, or quick, way to respond to your customers."

The room turned silent and glum at the memory of that event. Lee motioned to Sherm to move to the next slide. "That's why your senior leadership had the foresight to create a 'Plan B,' just in case there were any issues. After the debacle at the kick-off, they decided to implement Plan B and engaged my company to back you up. We will be hosting the CET application for you. And when CET is as successful as we all know it will be, the risks of you exceeding your immediate capability to deliver service, and impacting your users, will become no more than a bad memory."

Helena, the Director of infrastructure services, interrupted Lee. "Isn't hosting kind of dot-com era nonsense? We do have sufficient data center space to support the application. What are you adding that we can't provide"?

Lee paused, smiled, and looking directly at her, said, "Hosting was a big thing during dot-com, but this is different. We're not just racking your equipment, applications, and providing feeds and speeds. We will actually be providing the CET application to you and your customers. We're providing the entire software experience to your customers ... everything from delivery of functionality, to support for incidents, and escalated support questions. We're going to give you the capability to provision more or less capacity by yourself ... on demand. You'll be able to check the status from everywhere, through almost any kind of properly secured device. We'll give you the ability to rapidly increase or decrease the level of service we provide. And most importantly, we will measure usage, and only charge you for what you use. That's a big improvement over building out capacity that sits idle, waiting, just in case you need it. We will treat CET as if it was our own. We will provide you and your customers with an end to end turnkey solution for CET ... turning it into Software as a Service ... SaaS. That will free your teams up to concentrate on what they do best, and spend less time worrying about what level of resources is required to support CET capacity. We work for you."

I was impressed that Lee didn't shoot Helena down. In fact, he acknowledged her contribution. He had taken her attempt to derail him and worked it into his message.

Helena shook her head. "It's not secure to have all of that customer information, and our proprietary applications, floating around out there where anyone can hack into it. Do you have any idea of the legal and financial impacts of a breach at your site? And don't tell me it won't happen, because commercial companies are probed every day, especially those providing Cloud services. They're such a rich target, they attract attacks."

Lee nodded his head. "Absolutely correct. Which is why we have a very large security staff ... some of the best in the business from around the world ... most with extensive government three letter agency and military experience." Lee paused for a moment. I'd seen this move before. The man knew how to be dramatic. "And even some who used to make their living hacking into businesses just like yours, and getting away without being noticed. When you want to protect yourself against criminals, it helps to know a little about how they think."

Ahmed, the Director of customer support, pointed his finger at Lee and said, "And how do you intend to learn all you need to know to manage CET for us? Where will you get the experience we've built up over the years with our customers and their needs? And that's not to mention that since you're doing all this work for us, what about pending layoffs, as a result of the loss of work here? What happens to all of those people, and their families"?

The room went immediately silent at the mention of the word layoff. Everyone seemed to be holding their breath. Jessica broke the silence. "Executive leadership is committed to minimizing distractions for our company's employees, so they can focus on what they do best for the customer. And while the needs of the business can change, there are no plans for any reductions in force, or hiring freezes, as a result of this activity. Any additional resources freed up by this, will be deployed to advance additional requests from our business partners in other areas. To put it bluntly, we have more really fun and cool work available than we have people. Rest assured, you will not be wanting for something to do."

Lee turned off the laptop. "And Ahmed, we want to learn the best way to support you and your customers directly from you and your teams ... the people who are the experts. While my company has a proven, robust and sustainable methodology for delivering our Cloud services, we will also be in frequent contact with members of your teams, to ensure we are covering the right areas. I've asked for, and your CIO has approved, a representative from your company to share the responsibility with my company. He will also be accountable to you for the performance of the CET application."

Lee turned and gestured toward me. "Both Jessica and I agreed, that based on prior experience, Chris would be the best person to serve as liaison between my company and your company. I hope your teams will all extend to Chris the support needed to make this a rapid success."

Sean leaned over and whispered. "I'd buff up my resume if I were you. I don't see you getting out of this alive."

Tips that would have helped Chris

1. It is common that you will not be involved in the actual negotiation of supporting arrangements with third parties. In those cases, you will be dependent on the quality of the agreement as negotiated. Focus on working within the agreement, not what you would have done differently.
2. IT is a much smaller industry than we think. It is common that people from your company may leave and at some time in the future re-engage, but from the other side of the table. Sometimes there are time-based contractual restrictions on this, but it is better to assume, as lawyers do, that someone on your side of the table may be on the other side at some point in the future, or vice versa. This is another reason not to burn bridges.
3. A major risk to successful capacity management can be the over reliance on historical trend analysis to determine estimates of future needs. Capacity needs tend to increase step-wise, rather than in a linear fashion, and are often driven more by the introduction of new activities, rather than the simple, organic growth of existing activities. Robust capacity management estimates are built up each time anew, rather than simply being extensions of the past.

CHAPTER 4: THE ABANDONED SERVICE

My first stop was with Keshav. He was the Director of the development groups that produced CET. As we approached his office, I turned to Lee and said, "I hear he is smart, really smart. He's got multiple masters degrees from UC Berkeley, a PhD from MIT, and started post-grad work at Stanford when he was only 23, and all in subjects that I don't even know what their names mean. He's so intelligent that the rest of us are about as bright as carrots compared to him."

Lee's expression never changed and his stride never faltered. "There are many kinds of intelligence," he said. "Some are highly valuable in business and others are no more than intellectual curiosities. Everyone has a different type of intelligence. The trick to good leadership is identifying what type of intelligence is needed for a particular situation, and putting the person with the complementary intelligence in the lead. That's why we use team selling. And note that I said complementary type of intelligence. Using the same type of intelligence can often create only conflict."

He talked to me in the same tone one would use for a two year old child, and then gave me that forced smile I hated so much. "Don't be afraid, Chris. Just follow my lead and you may actually learn something, if you can keep your mouth shut and your eyes open."

"I'm hardly afraid, Lee," I said. "You should know better …"

He held his finger up and said, "Just listen and observe."

Just as I started to open my mouth to say something about Sherm's absence, Lee's phone buzzed discreetly. He scowled as he read the text.

"Sherman is once again stuck in traffic. Hiring him was a mistake. If he hadn't been the nephew of one of the members of the Board of Directors, I doubt he would have even been interviewed. That's why I am going to make him your primary contact. I think it will improve your skills if you have to improve his. Think of it as the blind leading the blind."

For a moment I thought about protesting, but decided not to. Jessica and Ricardo had made me our company's contact for Lee's company, and it was my job to work with whomever they assigned to us. There was no way I could win that fight and avoid Sherm. It could only hurt me.

We reached Keshav's office, and without waiting to be invited, Lee entered and sat down in a chair on the other side of Keshav's desk. He motioned for me to sit beside him, and raised his index finger to his lips to remind me to stay silent and observe.

Keshav seemed oblivious to our presence, and looked every bit the Hollywood stereotype of a full-on computer geek. One entire wall of his office, from floor to ceiling, was covered in erasable white board and filled with diagrams, calculations, and long bulleted lists in a variety of colors. On the other side of his large wooden desk, Keshav picked at two different computers, while carrying on a rapid argument on a speaker phone about some aspect of systems design that I couldn't understand. On his desk were a stack of vendor documents and proposals, as well as several well used and unwashed coffee mugs. One looked like it could detect Wi-Fi signals; another was etched with the symbol for a caffeine molecule. A third looked like a small Tiki statue with red LEDs in the eyes that kept blinking on and off. I couldn't see any mold inside them, and somehow I found that a little reassuring.

The credenza behind Keshav was stacked with papers, old dusty binders and an entire shelf of strange little toys, each more unusual than the next. Some had solar panels, others seemed to have batteries and multiple legs. One even had a small LED screen.

After a few moments, Keshav dropped off the call and began making notes in a hard-backed composition book with numbered pages. The last time I saw one of those, I was still in college.

Despite Lee's admonition to sit quietly, I spoke up first. I knew from experience that Lee could not be trusted. And now as a vendor, he had even more reason to throw me under the bus anytime it was to his advantage.

As I began to ask some initial questions, Lee slid his business card across the desk until it rested near the notebook Keshav was using, and then he started talking over the top of me.

"Thank you very much for meeting with us today, Keshav. I know you only by reputation, and it is quite formidable to say the least," said Lee. "Before we rush into questions, if you would be willing to share a little about what your team is working on … on a simple level that both Chris and I can understand … I would greatly appreciate it."

Keshav ignored both of us and continued writing. Only when he closed his notebook did he look up. He opened a drawer in his desk and pulled out a box. The box was full of vendor business cards … at least 100 of them. He dropped

Lee's in, shook the box, and then dumped all the cards into a pile on the desk between us. "And those are only last month's cards. But I'm very fair to all vendors, no matter how puerile their approach or proposal may be. I treat them all the same."

He swept the cards across the desk with his arm, and they tumbled into the box. He put the box back in the drawer. As he closed the drawer, he looked directly at me and spoke. "Chris, I've got a team meeting in 15 minutes, so this needs to be quick and focused."

I thought I could see a tiny curl of dissatisfaction on Lee's face, and I enjoyed it. "During our assessment of the CET situation, there were some questions asked that we could not answer. Unfortunately, there was no one from your development team who was able to attend, so we were hoping you could help us out."

Keshav nodded. "I do not require my team to attend these process meetings. While our work processes are quite structured, much of what we do requires a strong creative element. When a useful creative thread appears, it must be followed. Otherwise, it will be lost. And the results of that activity are usually far more valuable than the results of finger-pointing at someone who forgot to fill out the right form. You have to remember we are here to produce real products, not argue with the uninformed about which documents get filled out first."

I suppressed a chuckle. I know I sure felt that way some times.

I said, "There were some concerns that during the design and development, the CET app had not been thoroughly evaluated for the impact it would have on our environment.

The testing team reps indicated that there weren't sufficient hooks in the application for them to fully test it. They showed us copies of the design documents, and pointed out how allowances had been made for unit testing and some validation testing, but there was nothing included for integration or system testing. Can you educate me on your team's role in including the appropriate hooks in the application to facilitate testing, and their role during testing, before the product is released into production"?

Keshav began collecting some documents for his next meeting as he spoke. "Look, Chris, I know you're not an architect, so I can't expect you to fully understand all of the factors that go into sizing the needs of an application with the complexity of CET. You don't have the technical background or experience. So just think about this."

Keshav pulled up some charts on his tablet and spun the tablet across the desk to me. The charts seemed to cover the last two years and showed a red line near the top of the page, with multiple, colored lines near the bottom.

"We haven't even begun to reach the limits of what our infrastructure environments should be able to handle. Despite what those knuckle-draggers over in infrastructure want to believe about how lean and mean they operate; they aren't. We're no better than most other companies. On a normal day, we use barely 40% of our available storage space and less than 20% of our computing power. That's the curse of distributed computing … waste. But with the cost of physical equipment plummeting every year, it's not very expensive waste … as long as it's on a small scale."

I nodded and made some notes. "Did you use any kind of special tool to figure out what CET would need to be a success … that it would not exceed our capabilities"?

Keshav gave a heavy, almost theatrical sigh, and shook his head, as if I were too stupid to understand his message. "You mean did we measure it once it was built? Like in some kind of simulation before we released it for testing? Of course not. How could we run something we hadn't created before to see if it would work in our environment, without risking impacts to production? Surely you have some operational experience and understand the potential impacts application errors may have on the active business."?

"But isn't that what our testing team is for? I'm wondering how your team assisted them. Doesn't the testing team have a setup that allows you to test your team's work, in an environment identical to our production environment"?

Keshav pulled the tablet back and called up a series of pie charts. He pointed to the utilization data. "Our infrastructure team provides the company with a rather antique environment. It's flat, open and integrated ... not to mention needlessly gigantic. It bears the hallmarks of its mainframe roots, rather than having been updated to our current distributed computing focus in development. To fully test a new application, we'd need a test environment the size and capability of our full production environment. And no one is going to fund a duplicate production environment that sits idle most of the time."

Keshav raised himself up in his chair and stiffened his posture. "You have only been here a little time, Chris. And you have almost no knowledge of application architecture. I expect you to ask those kinds of ignorant questions. I've been successfully doing this kind of work for over ten years, and I assure you our company has so much excess capacity, CET will reduce the amount of waste. Finally, some equipment will shift doing nothing more than generating heat and consuming electricity, to actually be productive."

He stood up, as if to emphasize his point even more. "Even a blind man could see we have plenty of room to roll out this application and improve the utilization of the company's assets. There is nothing wrong with our design, or our determination of what it requires in our environment. Our design will actually improve the utilization and efficiency of the company's IT environment. If you want to know where the fault lies, I suggest you go inspect the quality of our infrastructure and the people who operate it."

"Do you gather any statistics about the actual impact of the application on available capacity once it is released into production ... anything that could be used as feedback for future development projects"? I asked.

"Once we release the product, and it is accepted into production, our obligation ends. Oh, we do make ourselves available during the first 30 days of operation, in case the infrastructure people get confused, or if they get questions they can't answer because they weren't paying attention when we trained them. But we follow best practice ... and we are not so arrogant to think we should deviate from industry best practice. It's up to the operational infrastructure people to monitor the overall usage of the application, and if they need more infrastructure, they should of course order it. But I'm not going to tell them how to run their business, even though what happened at the kick-off is a good example of the kind of work they do."

"Does that kind of failure happen often when a large, new product is released into production"? I asked.

Keshav laughed and stood up … grabbing his materials off the desk. "While that is a question better put to the infrastructure teams, I believe the answer is no. The company wouldn't be here if it were true."

As he walked around the desk and headed for the door, Keshav said, "Time's up. I'm leaving. Please do not play with any of my toys … you break it, you bought it. And remember to close the door on your way out. By the way, Chris, this has been really refreshing. It's been a long time since I have been asked so many ignorant questions with such earnestness."

A moment later he was gone, leaving just Lee and myself in the room.

Lee was calm on the outside, but I knew he was seething on the inside. He hated to be ignored, or treated like he wasn't the most important person in the room. Maybe working with Lee's company on this project might be fun after all.

We both stood up and I headed for the door, but Lee walked behind Keshav's desk. He stared at the shelf full of Keshav's toys for a moment, then selecting the most complicated and delicate seeming one, he pulled it from the shelf, raised his arm as high as he could reach and let it crash into the garbage can beside the desk.

Lee came up beside me and I said, "Keshav said not to touch his toys."

Lee put his arm around my shoulder and said, "Looks like you didn't respect that and broke one. Now you're going to have to buy him a new toy."

"You broke it, not me," I said.

4: The Abandoned Service

Lee said, "I'm not worried about paying for a new one because he's going to believe it was you and you will get the pleasure of paying for it. And I will get the pleasure of watching you learn a lesson about respect."

Lee laughed as I stood there stunned.

Tips that would have helped Chris

1. An enormous challenge to effective capacity management is when dealing with environments which due to design or scale, make resource sharing difficult, even with quickly burstable Cloud-based resources. Distributed in-house computing environments encourage the view of an environment as a network of iconoclastic mini environments.

2. Capacity management is not something you do once a month. You should be constantly measuring thresholds at an appropriate level of detail. Statistical process control can be of great help in interpreting the results.

3. It is very possible that the design of your environments may be of a scale and complexity such that they cannot be tested as an integrated service before being sent to production. This can be a dangerous situation. Your best alternative is to integrate as many components as can be tested and evaluate them in groups, until you have covered the entire service. Many third parties will require testing of your service before they accept it into whatever Cloud capabilities you've contracted for. The last thing they want to do is accept a service that will not operate properly and cause them to miss their contractual commitments.

CHAPTER 5: DON'T CONFUSE ME WITH THE DETAILS

At Sean's suggestion, I'd arranged time with Aphra, who'd been the project manager for CET. Of all the people involved, I was sure she would have the most end to end view at a detailed level. Although the application was going to be part of a Cloud environment with Lee's company, I still wanted to understand the whole thing. I wanted to know that someone ... somewhere, had considered the complete capacity requirements for CET. And if she had no concerns with that, hopefully she could at least point out some potential weak spots for me to address. I just wanted to get this done and go back to my regular work. The only way that could happen was if I found something to fix and took care of it. I didn't think Ricardo and our leadership would care too much if that was the final word. They just wanted to see some action, so they could go back to their duties too.

I showed up at her cube at the agreed-upon time, but she was nowhere to be found. I tried asking the people nearby if they knew where she was, but they had no idea. I'd been waiting for about 15 minutes, and was about to give up, when Aphra came quick-walking down the corridor. She was not very tall, which made the binders stuffed to bursting with papers, as well as the two bound notebooks she carried, seem all the larger a load. Interestingly enough, I couldn't see a laptop or tablet. She was probably the first person I'd ever seen here without one firmly attached to them. It was almost as if she were living in a pre-digital age.

"Hi," she said. "I'm Aphra. Sorry I was late, but we had the kick-off for a new project and there were lots of questions I needed to ask and answer." Without waiting for my reply, she said, "You must be Chris. Come on in." She gestured to her cube and said, "Mi casa es su casa."

Rows of neatly labeled binders filled the shelves of her bookcase. Aphra carefully found the right spot for each of the binders she was carrying, and put them back where they belonged. The notebooks went into her desk, except for one, which she carefully arranged in the corner of the desk just to her left. She pulled her phone and scanned through what I assumed was her e-mail and other messages. Apparently satisfied nothing critical had happened during her walk back from the meeting, she set her phone down and said, "So how can I help you, Chris"?

"You're very busy," I said. "I will do my best to keep this brief. I know you were the project manager for CET. We're in the process of establishing the operations of CET in a third party supplied and managed Cloud environment, since we seem to be having capacity issues running it in our existing infrastructure environment and we can't afford to have any more service delivery issues like we've already seen. I was hoping you could answer a few questions, or direct me to the right people to answer them."

Aphra spun her chair around and pulled down a fat binder stuffed with paper and plopped it on the desk in front of her. "Whatever you need."

"We've identified the common element of the service disruptions as being due to capacity in our infrastructure. We're concerned we didn't see any of these issues coming. They seem to have popped in out of the blue. Clearly, we are not adequately monitoring CET's capacity needs in real time. We're only doing it reactively and retrospectively. Can you share with me what was discussed, and what was implemented in terms of the breadth of capacity monitoring for CET … its frequency, breadth and reporting"?

Aphra didn't open her binder. "That's pretty specific information you're looking for, you know. Maybe you should speak to the individual subject matter experts to get their perspective."

"I could do that, but there were quite a few people involved. I know CET is complex and involves a lot of elements. I was hoping that, as project manager, you could provide me with a broader end to end perspective."

Aphra sat back in her chair. "I'm sure that would be great to have, but I don't really get involved in the detail. That's up to the SMEs. I prefer to manage projects at a higher level. It ensures I don't get in the way of the operational teams doing their jobs."

"Yes, but I'm sure you have a detailed project plan. That would be a help."

"You're not a project manager here at this company, Chris. So I don't think you truly appreciate what our role is. I facilitate the introduction of the need, and help inform the SMEs. Usually the need is presented by someone from the organization requesting the work … typically one of our business partners. Once that's in place, I work very hard to not get in the way of the different SMEs."

"I understand that," I said. "But who coordinates the activity? There are a lot of moving parts, especially with an application as complex as CET. Isn't that your role"?

"Our culture is based on the idea that we are all adults, and all focused on our collective success, above all. To help that happen, we try to avoid wasted or redundant effort. The best way to do that is to avoid over-managing work or duplication. When a need is presented, I arrange for a wide selection of SMEs to participate in the review. It's usually a large list because I need to make sure nothing is missed. Because they're all adults working for the common good, I don't need to tightly oversee what they do. The teams that need to participate will self-identify who they are, what they will do, and the schedule they will work under. Amongst them, someone will naturally step forward and declare themselves to be the overall coordinator. That owner may step down and another take their place as the project moves along. That ensures we always have the best leader in place for the project, and keeps the various SMEs from stepping on each other's work. As long as each does a great job in their area, the results will be exceptional. My role is to aggregate their timelines, collect any information the SMEs have to update their progress at a group level, and then further summarize it into something appropriate for leadership."

I shook my head. I had never heard of a project manager who worked like that. And while I hadn't been involved in the development of new applications at this company before, what Aphra was talking about was completely different from anything I'd seen elsewhere.

"Summing that all up," I said. "You're telling me that when a request comes in for something new, you gather everyone together into a room, leave, assume they will figure it out, and that someone will step forward and take ownership of the entire project"?

"That's a little bit superficial." Aphra pulled a sheet from the binder. It was a slide with a timeline and a couple of lines running across it. There was a stoplight image in the upper corner, with the green light lit up. "This is what I prepared for leadership each week. It let them know everything was under control and that we'd make the date agreed upon by the development and operationalization teams. My role is not to oversee the detail. So I don't spend any time on it. My role is to communicate with leadership."

As I looked at it, I understood how it could be appropriate as a one page summary for leadership of the project status. But I felt like someone either had gotten lazy or missed the point. Someone had decided that if leadership wasn't looking at the detail, nobody else had to. And because the operational teams didn't want anyone judging their performance, they didn't report any details outside their teams.

"Tell me, Aphra," I asked. "How long has this methodology been in place"?

"I don't know. At least seven years, because that's when I started here, and it was fully in place then. But you should see this slide when it's presented. The stoplight is all animated with blinking lights. I think that really grabs the audience."

"Can you at least tell me about the types of metrics that were planned to measure the status of capacity supporting the application? Surely that must have been discussed. With an application as complex as CET, the only way you could measure its capacity performance would be to watch each of the component elements within it. I'm concerned how we're going to do that if the application is migrated to a Cloud environment of any kind."

Aphra put her binder back on the shelf. "I wouldn't know about that. I think that given our culture, you should probably start with each one of the operational teams and find out how they measure capacity for their area."

I still couldn't believe what she was telling me. "I assume you understand that this is only as strong as its weakest link. It doesn't help if everyone has capacity for additional volume spikes, if there is one operational group that does not. We're delivering an end to end service, not a group of products from each individual functional group. From our customer's perspective, the service is much more than just the sum of the individual components."

"Now you are being philosophical, I think," she said. "It's like a fine watch. As long as everything is there, it will work. There are no magic parts that appear when everything is put together. We're just more efficient about it because we don't over-manage, and avoid duplication of effort. It works for us. Besides, that's what our 30 day critical care process is about. It lets us work out any issues once the service is in operation and delivering for our customer."

I thought about saying something about how well it doesn't work, given we've already had several serious failures since the service was launched, and letting the customer debug it for us was not a great strategy, but decided that wouldn't change anything.

"Besides ..."

Aphra never finished her sentence. The phone rang and she immediately answered. After a moment, she said, "I really need to take this call, Chris. I hope I've been able to help you. I can send you a list of all of the functional groups involved, and their leaders, so you can interview each of them individually." She handed me a list of names and functional areas.

There was no way I was going down that road, especially since I doubted I'd get anything beyond what Aphra had already given me. "Thanks a lot, Aphra," I said, standing up and heading out. "I really appreciate the help."

As I walked into the corridor, I scanned down the list and then stopped when I got to testing, the lead SME on that was Claire. That had potential. If they did system testing or performance testing there should be data on how the application performs as volumes ramp up.

It was time to go visit Claire. But first, I needed some coffee and there was a break room just up ahead.

When I walked in the room was empty except for one other, sitting facing the wall on the far side of the room. As I filled my cup, I realized it was Sherm, Lee's understudy, and the person who had that terrible presentation for our leadership.

I walked over and stood beside the table. He was furiously scribbling words into a notebook. The screen of his laptop was full of presentation slides.

"Hi, Sherman. Remember me, I'm Chris. I was at your presentation to our leadership."

He looked up, although wouldn't make eye contact, and said, "It's just Sherm. Only my mother calls me Sherman, and that's when she's angry with me …"

"And Lee calls you Sherman," I interrupted.

"Yeah, and he's always angry with me, too."

I sat down at the table. "Don't feel bad. He was always angry with me, and even now, after I no longer work for him, he's still angry with me. It's nothing specific. I think he does it on general principles, as if he believes it will make people better if he is always on their case."

Sherm gave a half-snicker, half-snort, which seemed to pass for his concept of a laugh, and stopped working.

"How long have you worked for him"? I asked.

"Almost two months now," said Sherm.

I nodded. "Well you're doing well then because he usually puts people on performance improvement plans before they even get to 30 days."

"Well, he's threatened it a lot and the way he yelled at me after the presentation I gave to your leadership, I thought he was going to put me on one for sure."

I nodded. "Sounds like Lee. Sorry for your situation. When can you transfer to another manager, or another role at your company"?

"Lee would have to allow the transfer, and he would never do that. He'd probably think it would reflect poorly on him if people left working for him instead of clamoring to be part of his team."

"You mean you actively fought to work for him"?

"That's what I told them, but I didn't really mean it. I was just desperate for work. I hadn't gotten a paycheck in almost two years. The only thing I could find were jobs working in fast food at minimum wage. I was desperate. And since they had been looking to fill that slot for a while, I went for it. I figured I could tolerate any manager for a year and then I would have a base from which to move on."

"I understand. That's how I felt when I found an opening here at this company. I just didn't choose Lee. I had him pressed upon me when my previous manager was let go."

"They seem to do a lot of firing at your company. Not that they don't at my company. Maybe it just seems that way because the numbers are bigger."

"They do a lot of it here. The way it was explained to me, off the record, was that there is a cultural philosophy that managers should cull the bottom ten percent of the people in their team each year, and bring in fresh blood that are expected to be better than the ones that were let go. The belief is that by doing so, it will advance the quality and performance of the entire workforce."

"Wow ... but I guess it's not too far from my company," said Sherm. "We have a lot of churn in people. Maybe that's why Lee likes it."

Sherm's phone lit up with a text. He took one look and said, "That's Lee. I've got to go now."

"No problem," I said. "It's good to get to know you a little better."

Sherm actually tried to smile and said, "It's even better to meet a kindred spirit."

Tips that would have helped Chris

1. If you are managing a relationship with a Cloud provider, make sure you establish some back channel contacts outside of the formal contract relationships. Get to know some kindred spirits as people, and not just as suppliers. Occasionally, there will be situations where you need something very minor but slightly off contract, as will they. These back channel relationships will help you develop a working relationship, which can be more powerful than a contractual relationship.

2. When you begin your capacity and availability process project, you will find that every company has its own approach. Don't be tied to a single methodology. You may find that your current company's approach is weaker than what you are accustomed to. Try to remember that your task is not to upgrade project processes. Your task is to get capacity and availability operational. Work with what's available if you want to make your schedule.

3. Assume that your project manager has no understanding, and no interest, in understanding how your capacity and availability processes work. Offer to share the information with them, and if they are interested, it is very worthwhile to educate them.

CHAPTER 6: VOICES IN THE NIGHT

It was wonderful.

Clear, sunny skies punctuated by fluffy clouds, drifting along like cotton puffs. The sun was warm and comforting as I lay on the grass beside a gurgling stream. No worries … no cares … nothing to cause me any concern. No computers. No pagers. No alarms. Time seemed to have passed everything by. All was wonderfully relaxing.

Paradise was interrupted by an old-fashioned pay phone that suddenly appeared by my feet and began endlessly ringing. A wooden wall phone with a crank appeared beside me and began ringing, then a rotary desk phone beside it. All manner of antique phones began popping up like a time lapse movie of dandelions in the spring. I tried hanging them up, but there was no one on the line and they would not stop ringing.

A moment later, my eyes popped open. The room was bathed in the soft, blue glow of my clock. On the end table my cell phone was ringing and vibrating so hard I thought it would work its way over the side and onto the floor.

I sat up, rubbed my face, and hit the speakerphone button on the device. At first I thought it was morning already and I needed to get to work, but I had second thoughts when I checked the clock and it read 2.17 am.

I'm slow to wake, and even when my eyes were open, it took me a while to engage my brain. The best I could manage was a stumbling, "Yeah"?

"This is Ricardo. Please call in to the conference bridge number I just texted you. We're having our first severity one service disruption with CET since Lee's company took over. I need you in the war room now."

I rubbed my face and tried to shake the cobwebs out of my head. I dialed the number and kept the phone on mute as I yawned, while a jumble of background voices came through from the other side.

Ricardo sent me another text telling me that Lee was not answering his phone and he was trying to manage the virtual war room, which was quickly becoming a tug of war between my company's IT teams and the technical and operational staff of Lee's company. Neither group felt accountable for the situation and were pointing speculative fingers at each other. No one had any idea what needed to be done, but both groups felt they were the only ones who could resolve it and fix what were obviously the mistakes of the other group. It was fast becoming the technical equivalent of the "not me" game.

Ricardo was trying, without success, to create enough order so he could check attendance and collect a master list of who was on the call. I wasn't sure why I was on the call, or why Ricardo was acting like an incident manager. Where was the incident lead from Lee's company? They were supposed to coordinate ownership and communication to leadership regarding any issues relating to CET disruptions. Everyone else was a technical specialist of one sort or another, whose job was to get the service restored as fast as possible. I probably shouldn't have been surprised. Normal procedure for many things at our company was different from what I'd ever seen elsewhere, but in the absence of action by Lee's company, people fell back into the way they were used to managing events like this ... get everyone and anyone who might remotely have some interest involved, even if there is no possibility of them being needed. That way leadership couldn't be accused of missing something. Any failures would be on someone else's head. And as the issues clarified, those people best suited to resolve them would rise to the occasion and lead the rest of the people in the solution creation and implementation. At least that was the theory. I'd never seen it work. But then again, this was the only place I'd heard of that model.

Ricardo was starting to sound a little frayed around the edges from trying to control all the personalities on the call, when I got a text from Sherm. It simply said, "I'm listening to call. Lee is on a flight. He has no phone service. Trying to get someone else to fill in till he lands in three hours."

I immediately sent him a reply. "No! You take over now. It's what we pay your company for."

Without reading Sherm's reply text, I broke into the chatter on the call and said, "A representative from Lee's company is coming onto the call. His name is Sherm. He will be incident manager for this event. It is one of the services we contracted for from the company as part of our migration of CET to their Cloud environment." Sherm was a nice guy and I hated to put him on the spot, but he was going to own this whether he liked it or not.

With a sound of relief in his voice, Ricardo added, "Please give Sherman your complete cooperation."

A moment later Sherm stumbled into the conversation, coughing and sniffling his way through introducing himself. As Sherm tried to restore order in the room, my home phone rang. It was Ricardo. While he talked, I filled a mug with the cold and stale remnants of yesterday's coffee and popped it into the microwave. It was bad enough drinking day old coffee, but to drink it cold was the worst.

"Something is seriously wrong here," said Ricardo. "I'm told that the servers supporting the Cloud at Lee's company aren't down and the network is functioning fine, but services to use are not accessible to us, or anyone else, remotely. Jessica just called. Apparently, the CEO found out about it from the business before IT did, and called her before she knew it was going on. I'm sure Jonah, our CEO, doesn't like getting told by one of our customers about a problem, and being in the position of knowing nothing about it. I know when Jessica couldn't reach Lee she called the head of Lee's company. He keeps insisting this is not a major issue."

I was just sipping the first cup when Sherm gained enough control of the call for the Head of third shift IT operations to be heard over the background chatter. He started trying to explain what had happened. It was clear, even to me, that he was just guessing. With the entire application in Lee's Cloud, there wasn't much else he could do but guess. All he could tell us was that no services were being delivered. I was awake enough to know that guessing was exactly the wrong thing to do. To make matters worse, the technical SMEs from Lee's company were insisting they could find no problem in their infrastructure or network, so they felt strongly that the issue must be one of our design, or something else internal to the application ... therefore out of their control and not covered by contract obligations.

Two minutes later I was swallowing the last of the coffee in my cup when Preston, our business VP, and Jonah, our

CEO, came on the call. The scary part was that neither asked any questions. But when Jonah began to speak, the entire room got silent. It was the quietest I'd ever heard a group of engineers who were focused on resolving an issue. First, Jonah apologized profusely to Preston on behalf of the entire company for the outage. Jessica jumped in the moment he finished. Not only did she apologize, she even groveled a little bit. Jonah then spoke to the entire call and said that if anything was needed to get service restored immediately, we should go ahead and get it.

"Let me make it crystal clear," said Jonah. "If you encounter any resistance or pushback on what you need to resolve this ASAP, I expect you to call me immediately and I will remove the barrier. Right now, remediating the damage done from this failure to provide adequate capacity to support CET, is the single most important thing in each of your lives. And it will remain so until this is resolved and back to normal ... and my expectation of all of you is that it will happen very soon. Rest assured, I shall hold each of you responsible for making that happen."

There was a moment of silence on the call before Jonah said, "Preston and Jessica, if you would be so kind as to join me on our own call in ten minutes, I would appreciate it. My administrative assistant is sending you the call-in information now. Does anyone on this call have any questions before the executive team signs off"?

In an attempt to demonstrate he was in control of the call, Sherm then said, "Anyone on the call want to say anything before leadership leaves"?

I cringed because I knew what was coming next.

Our technical team immediately began to point fingers at Lee's company. After editorializing how the decision to operate and support CET from a third party Cloud environment was a huge mistake, they began to speculate on what was wrong with the environment Lee's company provides. That immediately evoked a similar response from the SMEs at Lee's company, with added comments about how this was an area outside our expertise and best left to the experts, such as themselves.

As the clutter of voices on the call turned into unintelligible noise, Sherm tried desperately to get everyone's attention, to get people to be quiet. No one responded to him and the speculation and accusations continued to get worse.

Suddenly, Sean's voice cut through the clutter. He was very well respected across the company, and on hearing him, people began to quiet down, wanting to hear what he had to say.

"Something's not right here, folks. If you'd just stop covering you butts for a moment, it would be obvious. You're right in that this is something that is best left to experts, and all of the SMEs on this call are the experts. So first I want to apologize to leadership for the confusion. I'm personally embarrassed by the way everyone is focused on themselves and not on the customer. To Jonah, Preston and Jessica ... you all know me. I give you my personal assurances we will do everything possible to restore service immediately. We will provide you with updates every hour until service is restored. Additionally, we will reconvene a meeting tomorrow to let you know what happened and why, as well as what our remediation plan is going forward."

6: Voices in the Night

"Thank you, Sean," said Jonah. "Your leadership is very much appreciated. We all look forward to understanding the circumstances that caused this event. Preston ... Jessica ... if you will please join me on that other call."

After leaderships' phones clicked off the call, Sean said, "I'm sending all of you the link to a web meeting, where we can share, and look at some charts related to CET. I will see you all there in a moment."

There were a few laughs. At least I put my phone on mute while my laptop booted up. When people stopped showing up as logging into the meeting, Sean began.

"We've been running the capacity planning reviews for CET for the last three months," said Sean. "And you know what we found? Sherm, can you call up those charts"?

A moment later, charts of the utilization of resources by the CET application at Lee's company appeared. They covered the last three months. The charts were very familiar. We'd reviewed them every two weeks during our capacity management sessions. I was struck by how much they resembled the ones Keshav, the Head of Development, had shown us. They showed a red line near the top of the page with multiple colored lines representing CET resource consumption near the bottom.

Keshav had been right; the CET application needed very little capacity, even at full utilization ... whether in our environment or theirs. Something else was impacting our capacity. Were we measuring the wrong thing?

Tips that would have helped Chris

1. A service that is not available is worse than never having had the service at all. Don't forget that a service can be much more than just the interactions users have with it during the normal business day. It can include back office processing that occurs off hours and may be essential to providing the value of the service to the users.

2. Having third parties in a meeting where you are still gathering facts, can easily be a distraction. One method that works well is to have both sides gather their facts, and then reconvene with only the relevant players. Smaller groups get more done. You can keep others on call in case they are needed, but don't burn out your entire staff by making remediation of Cloud sourced services an extended group effort.

3. Although capacity and availability are tightly coupled, they do have a different focus. Understanding which is the immediate cause of the issue should be a top priority for these types of meetings.

CHAPTER 7: WHEN CAPACITY ISN'T ENOUGH

Being early for the meeting had the advantage of letting me choose my chair and its location; not to mention making sure the chair wasn't broken. Our conference rooms attracted broken furniture like engineers to a free lunch.

After the drama last night, this was definitely an important meeting, and those tended to last a long time, and I wanted to ensure I had a decent seat for the fireworks about to begin. At least if I had to spend the next hour or so in a dirty, worn-out room – a room jammed full of engineers, many of whom had been up all night.

I knew that per the company culture, while many were invited, few could be counted to physically appear. That's why I had mixed feelings about call-in numbers for the meeting. Sure, it was useful to someone who was out of town or in transit, but I knew from watching the people sitting around my cube that most of the time it was just people who were either too lazy to walk over to the conference room, or preferred to work on something else while they kept half an ear open to the meeting ... just in case they were assigned something.

Sean was next through the door. He had been around practically since the beginning and his fingers had been in almost everything IT had ever built or installed. I'd met him the first week I came onboard, and he always seemed to know the answer to any question I could ask.

Generally, I liked working with him. Sometimes it seemed like he supported what I was doing and sometimes it seemed like he was opposed to it. I could never tell until he started to act, and even then, it might change. It didn't mean he was indecisive. He just seemed to follow his own internal value system as to what was the right or the wrong thing to do in the situation.

Sean dropped his tablet down onto the table and threw himself into one of the old chairs. It was so wobbly that for a moment I thought it would fall over, but somehow he kept it upright.

"Did you have a nice rest last night"? I asked innocently. Sean had been on the call as long as I had.

"Nothing some intravenous caffeine wouldn't cure," he smiled. "Besides, I always get a tiny bit of pleasure out of telling arrogant, technical experts that their superior knowledge only extends to the limits of their discipline and not beyond."

Before I could probe that statement further, Sherm walked in.

"Where's Lee"? I asked. "Is he here or will he be one of those call-ins because he's off working on another account"?

Sherm dumped his materials on the table up near the whiteboard. "He'll be here. Don't worry." He started sorting through the documents and without looking up said, "Thanks for helping me out last night, Sean. I'm a little new to this and I'd never had to deal with such a raucous customer meeting before."

A moment later, Lee and Jessica silently walked in, one right after the other, and made a point of sitting on opposite sides of the table. Neither looked especially pleased.

Lee straightened his suit, brushing out a wrinkle with his hand. Finally satisfied at his appearance, he looked directly at Jessica and said, "I'm terribly sorry if there were any untoward events last night which may have impacted your user experience with the CET application."

Jessica snapped back, "That's a pretty lame apology, Lee. If you'd been there, you wouldn't have been so equivocal about whether there were any impacts. We lost an entire day's processing and that means we lost a day's billing and revenue."

Lee nodded and gesturing to Sherm, said to him, "Pull up that deck we got this morning from our office."

In through the door walked Preston … our business Vice President and owner of CET, and accountable to Jonah for the additional revenue needed to restore the year's financial results – the revenue he was counting on CET to deliver.

Lee immediately stood up, walked over to him, and offered his handshake. "Hi Preston, I hadn't expected you at this meeting, but it is always good to see you."

Preston scowled at Lee. "So what did your team do wrong last night, and how are you going to fix it so it doesn't happen again"?

Lee pointed to the capacity charts Sherm had displayed on the wall screen. "That's a great segue, Preston. I put our team of technical specialists to work on this last night, as soon as we realized something was wrong."

"You mean after I called because my teams were complaining that it was broken? Is that how IT finds out about the status of its applications … wait till the customer complains"? snapped Preston.

Lee strode up to the wall screen, an air of confidence and command about him. "If you will have a seat, Sean, I believe I can address Preston's concerns and our conclusions."

Preston shook his head. "I don't have time for this. I don't have time for service outages and I don't have time for you."

Without breaking a sweat, Lee said, "We can share this information with you any way you wish that fits best with your needs. May I suggest that since you are already here, why don't we take a look at this together. If you need to leave before we are done, I will be happy to work however is best for you."

Preston shook his head. "Go ahead. And get to the point."

Lee stood at the head of the room and began. "We've been tracking the CET application on our systems for some time now and reviewing that information with your company's technical team during our joint capacity management meetings. If you remember, there was a great concern during the establishment of our contractual relationship about my company's environments and whether we could provide the capacity to support CET and prevent these types of data log jams that take the system down, similar to what we saw yesterday. So once we received an alert of a potential untoward event we brought in our A-team of technical experts to conduct a deep and thorough analysis of the capacity demands CET has placed on our environment, relative to our capabilities."

Lee gestured and the first slide came up. It was nearly identical to the one we reviewed in each capacity management meeting, except it showed the information in much more detail, covering each hour for the last week. The available capacity was far beyond anything CET had ever used. Much as I hated to admit it, unless the chart was a bald-faced fabrication, Lee was right. There was nothing wrong with the capability of his company to provide us with capacity sufficient to support CET. Could he be right? If he was, that would mean the problem was somewhere inside the CET application itself. Or was it somewhere else?

"Our specialists looked at the application on an hour by hour basis and at no time did they find it even remotely close to the currently assigned capacity levels," said Lee.

Sean took a long, deep swig of coffee and snapped back, "That's wonderful ... absolutely brilliant. So how do you explain the outage of last night, or the others we've been having all the way back to the original kick-off? Is there an issue with your monitoring and operations teams"?

Lee just kept smiling. "Sean, I realize you weren't included in the rather rapid negotiations my company went through with your leadership in setting up this arrangement." He waved an arm in Preston's direction. "If you check with them I think you will find that they conducted extensive due diligence and were quite satisfied with what they found."

Sean shook his head. "But is that chart reflecting only our specific application, or does it also include other applications that may be in different virtual Cloud environments, but sharing physical space on your infrastructure? Are we getting lost in the averages"?

Lee never lost his composure. In fact, the more he was pressed, the more self-assured he seemed to become. "Just as your application and data are segregated and protected from other clients in our environment, so these analysis reflect only your company. My company operates based on best practice and will match anyone else in the industry in terms of our alignment and compliance with best practices. Our infrastructure experts are some of the best in the business, with an enormous collective number of years of service. We are supporting those key areas of concern your leadership expressed, and unlike many IT shops, we are focused on delivering the services our customers and users need in order ..."

Preston cut him off. "I don't give two rats what your experts say, or what your graphics show. What we need is very simple. It hasn't changed since our first meeting. We need services delivered on a dependable basis. That seems to mean having sufficient capacity to avoid the application crashing because there isn't enough capacity in the environment. I don't know the technical details, but I do know that we couldn't process customer billing last night and that puts the entire day's revenue at risk. And when our divisional sales teams discovered the application shutdown and contacted you ... note I said we discovered it, not you identified the problem and contacted us, you gave us this same speech. You need to take ownership of the problem and get it fixed immediately."

Pointing at Lee, Preston said, "Your job is easy. There are only four things you gotta do. First you gotta meet the service levels we both agreed to in the contract. Second, you need to be able to give us all the capacity we need. Third, you have to monitor the application performance and let us know when there is an issue, or the potential for an issue, before it impacts our operations. And fourth, you've got to keep showing us how you are doing a great job compared to where we were … and that doesn't mean spinning the data till it only looks good for you."

Preston didn't wait for Lee to respond. He turned and headed for the door. Stopping at the doorway, he turned back toward the room and said, "And while you are thinking about that, I will be speaking with legal about the contract terms relating to what constitutes non-performance, sufficient to terminate our agreement."

"You and I should have a conversation about this situation in the context of our long-term relationship," said Lee. "I can make myself free anytime that fits your schedule."

Preston ignored Lee's comment and started out the door. As he did, he said, "Oh, and let me add a fifth one to that list of four things. Stop wasting so much of my people's time," before slamming the door shut behind himself.

The conference room was so quiet that the sound of people breathing seemed as loud as a thunderstorm.

A text appeared on my phone. It was from Sherm. It simply said, "We need to meet if you wouldn't mind, please."

Tips that would have helped Chris

1. Cloud providers, or any other third party providers under contractual arrangement, will manage you and the delivery of services to that contract. Don't get distracted by trying to decide how to amend the contract when going through any problem management sessions. Focus on working with the contract. Amending the contract may take months. It can be included as part of the long-term remediation, but unless tabled for future review can be a material distraction.

2. Don't count on being able to change leadership opinions based solely on logic ... especially leadership outside of IT. Successful leadership is very results oriented. They will tend to view logic as promises and want to see results. Show them how it has worked, either at your company or elsewhere. Give them concrete examples and you will have much better luck.

CHAPTER 8: COFFEE TALK

I took Sherm out of the building to a coffee shop. We went to one nearby that I knew wasn't full of people from the company. It was one of the few stores still occupied in a slowly decaying strip mall. With the prior occupants of the empty storefronts forced out of business by the economy, there wasn't much rent left for the mall owner to maintain the facility. That was too bad. I liked the place because it was local ... not a chain. It also gave me a place to come when I needed to clear my head a bit and didn't want to be surrounded by people from the company, especially in the middle of the afternoon when they should all be hard at work.

And I had this idea that maybe if I got Sherm away from prying eyes for a few minutes, he might be a little more forthcoming about what was going on. Besides, they had free Wi-Fi.

With so many empty storefronts, we were able to park right by the door. Sherm hadn't said a word since we got into the car. He just sat there and stared out the window like a lost dog. It was very strange, but at least he hadn't insisted on dragging along those documents he always seemed to be carrying.

I held the door for him and Sherm walked into the coffee shop first. It was nearly empty. He stared at the floor for a while and when I didn't speak, he finally asked, "Where do you want to sit"?

"Let's get our drinks first, okay? I really need something to wake me up a little after all the hours we've put in over the last few days."

The server knew me and I barely had to start my order, when she said, "You want the usual, right? Large black coffee with a shot of espresso"?

I nodded with a smile, "Thanks."

Sherm stood silently beside me. Finally, I said, "You need to order what you want. Pick something from the list of beverages on the wall." I was trying to be supportive of his personality quirks, but there was no way I was going to order his drink for him, too. That was going too far.

Without even looking at the board on the wall with the list of drinks, Sherm said, "I'll have a medium Caffè Medici, if it isn't too much of a bother, please."

The server hesitated and said, "What"?

"If it is at all possible, I would really like a Caffè Medici. You know … double shot of espresso over chocolate syrup and orange peel … oh, and please don't forget the whip cream, if you have any."

The server smiled and said, "No problem. It sounds delicious. Maybe I'll make one for myself."

For a moment, it seemed like Sherm had personality … that he had some depth and intelligence to him, but then he fell back into the Sherm I had known at work.

"Where should we sit"? he asked, without looking at me.

"It doesn't matter," I said. "Just pick a spot."

Sherm shook his head. "That's okay. You know this place better than I do. You should pick."

"Okay. By the window," I said and pointed to a table with a great view of the parking lot and not too far from the door.

Sherm sat down and stared at the table, never once making eye contact.

We sat drinking in silence for a moment. I was testing to see if he just needed more time before he opened up, but nothing seemed to be happening, so I spoke anyway.

"So why did you bring me here, Sherm"?

"I didn't bring you here. You picked the place, remember"?

"Sherm, I'm really getting tired of this submissive, passive aggressive behavior. Whether you like it or not, we have to work together to get this thing working, and working well. And let me be very blunt. While there may be some data that suggests the issues are not at your end, the extent of your company's partnering with us seems to extend only as far as promptly cashing our checks."

For the first time, Sherm looked up and actually made real eye contact. "I can say something just as bad about your company. Did your leadership perform due diligence sufficient to confirm what Lee promised currently exists for others, and let you independently verify that it is being provided? Did you analyze what was appropriate to Cloud-out to us, or did you just dump everything on us so you didn't have to be accountable for the results? Did you do anything to independently monitor our performance? Did it ever occur to any of you that showing the same level of performance period over period is an enormous red flag ... either you're measuring the wrong thing, or the data is being managed."

I shook my head. "We gave it to you so we didn't have to monitor it. How can it make any sense for us to give it to your company if we still have to do all the work? And it makes zero sense to try to break the application up so you own part and we own part. That's just a guaranteed recipe for finger pointing, and a complete lack of accountability. Besides, we didn't have the time to build out the capacity the application needed."

Sherm shook his head. "But you had time to do it wrong. Ask yourself which is worse ... being late or being dysfunctional. Don't you realize that you're not just asking for infrastructure-as-a-service or platform-as-a-service. You asked for the highest risk and most impactful of all, software as a service – applications. I'll bet you still don't have a decent disaster recovery or business continuity program for your company, much less have the CET application integrated into those processes and tested."

From behind me, a voice said, "Sounds a little harsh to me."

I looked up and it was Sean walking past our table and up to the server behind the counter. "Ola, Magdalena. Got any coffee"?

She giggled and started working on a cup. "You want the usual? Giant Café Mélange and hold the milk, hold the foam"?

Sean nodded and picked the cup up from the counter when she was finished. He walked over to our table and without asking, simply sat down with us.

"What is that"? asked Sherm, pointing at Sean's drink.

"Black coffee. I just like to improvise."

"What are you doing here"? I asked. "This is my secret."

Sean laughed loudly. "I've been coming here since before all those other places in the mall went out of business. This used to be a company hangout in the early days ... I'm talking back when the entire IT department could all fit in here at once."

"Did you just park your dinosaurs outside"? I asked.

Sean laughed, snorted his coffee, and started coughing.

Sherm waited until Sean calmed down and then said, "Look, I am not supposed to meet with clients without Lee being present. My being here with you two could be justification in Lee's eyes to have me fired. I'm doing this because I think the relationship between my company and your company is unfair, and Lee is the force behind that. Lee is trying to squeeze as much out of your company for as little effort as he can. The more profit he shows on an account, the more money he makes."

"Hey," said Sean. "We're both in business to make money. No one forced us to sign up for this deal."

Sherm shook his head. "You don't understand, Sean. This isn't like the old days you always talk about. Lee would be elated if the failure of CET caused your company to collapse. He still feels he was not treated fairly while he was here."

"But why haven't you spoken up about this before? You're supposed to be our partners in this. We do well and therefore you do well. Why would you try to cheat us"? I asked. I couldn't believe they were trying to get as much from us as they could, while doing the least they could get away with.

Sherm started to respond, but Sean interrupted him. "They aren't cheating us. I can't believe you are so naive. They're simply managing to the contract. This is what leadership signed up for, which is how they developed a price for the service, and our company got suckered in by the lowest cost."

"Okay, so they are managing to the letter of the contract. But what about working together to the spirit of the contract"?

Sean shook his head. "You need to go out on some account calls with our sales team. How do you think we manage our customers? We price things consistent with what the customer wants. Is it fair for the customer to expect us to do more without an increase in revenue? Would you come to terms with someone to paint your house for a fixed price and then ask them to replace the roof while they are up there ... and do it without any additional cost to you"?

I slowly shook my head. Sean had a point, but he was missing that in a long-term business relationship, sometimes we ask them for a little extra and sometimes they ask us.

Sherm looked up and said, "I'm not going to contradict Lee, especially in public and never, ever, in front of a client. He put me on a performance improvement plan after what happened the other day. I have 90 days to become the person he wants me to be. If I do anything he doesn't like, the skids are greased for him to slide me out the door. And I cannot afford to lose this job. I'm pretty deep in debt and if I become unemployed again, I'd lose my house and probably be looking at personal bankruptcy. I'm taking an enormous risk just being here with you without Lee present. I'm trusting you by meeting with you now."

"Don't worry," I said. "What is said here, stays here. I know what it's like to be on Lee's hate list."

"Thanks," said Sherm. "Lee is ruthless and once he got your leadership to agree to a relationship that only looked at capacity and not availability of CET, he knew he had you."

"Huh," I asked. "Aren't they just different views of the same thing"?

"They have connections, but so do all of the ITSM related processes." Sherm spread out a napkin and started to draw on it.

"Availability management is the primary driver of customer satisfaction. But to do it right you've got to understand how the service supports the customer and the infrastructure that supplies it, on a component by component basis."

Sherm ran out of room on the napkin. He carefully folded it and put it in his pocket, before grabbing a fresh one. He drew three parallel lines and began marking off space on them.

"Imagine these are time lines. Availability management is all about improving the serviceability – the detection and restoration time, availability – how long it's been since service was restored and reliability – time between the onset of incidents. Services need to be designed with the capture of those measures in mind. You can't just add them on at the end. You've got to make availability part of the design requirements. Capacity and availability are related a little like problem and incident. They share elements, draw on some of the same data, but definitely have a different focus."

Sherm folded up the napkin and was about to put it in his pocket when I asked, "May I have that"?

He shook his head and finished putting it in his pocket. "Sorry, it's better if there are no notes. I'm just a little paranoid, but Lee will do that to you."

I smiled and nodded.

Sean said, "That's all fine in the theory department, but look at the realities. You keep showing us data on your company's performance that is clearly wrong, if for no other reason than it never varies in those reports you keep publishing."

"Think about the evaluation and negations between our companies," said Sherm. "Who was on the team from your side"?

"It was a very small group. Just our executive leadership," said Sean. "They needed to keep it a secret so it wouldn't cause disruptions in operations, or the marketplace. It would have much more positive impact if the launch came out of the blue. Besides, if they were going to have a technical person on the evaluation and negotiation team, I'd be the most logical one to ask. I've got more secrets than the entire lot of them combined, plus I built a lot of our infrastructure, so I understand its issues."

"That's not quite correct," said Sherm. "Lee insisted there be a technical representative from your company on the team. He pushed it because he didn't want anyone to think he was taking advantage of your company. He recommended Keshav because he knew the most about CET and had a good understanding of your environment. Lee said he had worked with him before and he'd be a good balance of knowledge and confidentiality."

"Now I am insulted," said Sean. "I hired Keshav into the company and he is a good architect, but he doesn't understand infrastructure that well."

"Jessica did bring up your name," said Sherm. "But Lee implied that while your knowledge was strong, he had concern in the areas of behaviors. Besides, Keshav was already working with Lee. They'd been discussing this for a while."

"What do you mean"? asked Sean.

"He was wired in to be the technical lead on your company's team," said Sherm. "Keshav and Lee had worked out a lot of the details of what would work before we even started pitching it to your company. I don't think everyone knew that … it never came up during the meetings, but I'd already done quite a bit of analysis and preparation for the presentation based on information Keshav had given Lee about CET, before we even walked in the door."

Sean shook his head. "I don't think that can be true. I know Keshav too well. He may be a flake, but he is not unethical."

"Besides, what would he get out of doing that? How could he benefit"? I asked. "I can't see anyone risking their job, and any future jobs in the industry, by doing that kind of thing."

Sherm shook his head. "I didn't realize you were so naive, Chris. I know Sean well enough to know he's a realist and I thought some of that might have rubbed off on you."

I looked at Sean and asked, "How well do you two know each other? I thought this was Sherm's first assignment for our company"?

Sean waved me off as Sherm said, "That's not important right now. You asked what's in it for Keshav. The answer is so simple. Think strategic and longer term than just one quarter. The CET project isn't about that one application to us. It's a proof point to show that much of IT can be sourced to third parties, such as Lee's company – even critical applications. If my company lived up to their end of the contract and CET was successful, then your leadership would be less resistant to moving virtually all of IT to our Cloud environments. That's Lee's goal. He only cares about CET as a proof point that gets him the opportunity to capture everything in IT. Your company then benefits by getting rid of all the IT people and expenses, and substituting the lesser costs of outsourcing everything to us.

But there would still be a few IT people left. Someone would need to represent the IT services in your company. That's what Lee promised Keshav. He'd get to be one of those people, and he would get to select who stayed and who left. Keshav is a very forward and practical thinker. He saw it as a matter of personal survival. It was the path that maximized his situation. He had arranged with Lee to push your company's IT teams out the door for his own benefit."

"Why are you telling me this"? I asked. "What's the benefit for you? I don't get it. Why would you take such a risk by telling us this"?

"Because I think what Lee is doing is wrong, and I know that he nearly got you fired here based on things he made up. So I thought you would appreciate knowing this. Your company is an important client to our company. Maybe this is a chance for you to show Lee what you really can do. If I am wrong and you don't have the heart, or the courage, to stand up for yourself and your peers, then forgive me for intruding. I will not mention it again, and will not think the less of you. I know you could lose your job if you speak up about this. And I wouldn't want to get you fired."

I looked at Sean and waited for some quip from him to break the tension, but he just sat there staring.

Finally, Sherm broke the silence and said, "I need to get back or Lee will start asking questions about my billable time." As we stood up, Sherm looked at me and said, "Remember what we said earlier. It's your choice. Do what you want. Just remember that when it comes to this conversation, not a word to anyone … please, or you will get me fired. "

Tips that would have helped Chris

1. Availability needs to be part of the service design. While capacity management can be appended later, without a way to measure and manage the availability for all elements of the service, you will have difficulty sustaining delivery for your users.

2. You need to look at the availability of not just the delivered end to end service. You must also consider the availability of the components that make up that service. If you do, when the end to end availability level bears investigation, you will be able to identify which aspect of the service needs attention.

3. When working with Cloud and other third party providers, always keep in mind that one of their objectives is often to expand the size and scope of their services you utilize to deliver services to your customers. This can be either through growth in your current service with them, or in expanding it to include other services you provide. There is nothing wrong with this. It is how they grow. But you should always view their actions through that lens.

CHAPTER 9: JUST SIT THERE AND TAKE IT

The next day I got an invite to a meeting with Ricardo, my manager, and I was late.

I bolted in through the entrance, flashed my ID at the guard and ran it through the ID scanner, then quick-walked to my meeting with Ricardo. With all the coffee I'd had in the last hour, it was all I could do not to run there, just for the fun of it.

Ricardo was sitting in his office waiting for me when I arrived. I think it was the first time he'd ever gotten to a meeting before me ... even his own meetings. Worse, he had the look of someone who'd just received a very thorough and professional beating by his management – everyone knows that look.

I didn't bother to knock. I just stepped into his office and sat down in a chair across the desk from him. "Hi, Ricardo. It's good to see you. What did you want to see me about"?

"Please close the door," he said. "We need to have a difficult conversation and I don't want it to distract others outside."

Now I knew this was going to be bad ... why I wasn't sure, but it was definitely going to be bad.

Some managers are "closed door" managers. Anytime they met one on one with someone, they kept the door closed. While part of that behavior was based on the need for some private conversations, I always felt that some of it was related to the need to show how important their conversations were.

Ricardo was an "open door" manager. He never closed the door to his office during a meeting. Most of the offices around his weren't occupied, so there weren't many people who might hear anything, except his admin, and she always knew everything.

Ricardo waited until I sat down before beginning. He was visibly angry. His normally, unflappable veneer had cracked. It was the first time I'd seen him so upset.

"You were assigned ownership of our relationship with Lee's company in their operational support of CET. You were assigned accountability for ensuring their performance. I met with Jessica and Preston a few hours ago and they are both very concerned that you have failed to put the right processes in place to ensure there is adequate capacity. As a result, they still don't feel we can rely on CET. Our infrastructure team has been lobbying quite successfully to bring the CET service back in-house because they would have more control of it. If it weren't for the accessibility requirements and capacity required of CET, we'd be looking at pulling it off the Cloud. And according to legal, we would still be accountable for the contractual payments to Lee's company. We are talking about not only missing our revenue targets for the year, but also negatively impacting the company's stock price, due to your failure. This impacts the company, its shareholders and its employees. According to my conversations with Lee earlier this week, and the information in your human resources file, you seem to have a history of not executing on your assignments. In fact, you nearly were asked to leave because of it. I know that Jessica gave you another chance and thought you had mended your ways. It appears you have not. She was very disappointed."

There it was. I knew it was coming. The moment Lee felt any risk or issues in the relationship, he was going to point the finger at someone else, and once again, it was me. That's why he had insisted I own the relationship. I was ready-made to take the blame, given what he'd done to me when I worked for him. Anyone who listened to his fabrications ... looked at what he had put in my file when he worked here ... who saw how Lee had put me on a performance improvement plan based on complete falsehoods ... could only come to the same conclusion Ricardo had. I couldn't really blame him.

"I don't understand what you mean"? I said, "Just today I met with Sherm and we discussed the current status of the project. Perhaps I should speak with Jessica and explain the situation to her."

"That would not be your best course of action at the moment."

"But we've been running trending analysis at our capacity management meetings. I've introduced statistical process control measures, to reduce the chance of getting blindsided."

"Have you been conducting stress tests of the application, or running simulations to verify the data we're receiving from Lee's company? Are you at least doing some quantitative modeling, to verify changes in demand aren't impacting the application and it continues to work as designed? What are you doing that we were not already doing to eliminate these capacity issues"?

"We met with Keshav, Head of the development team that designed and built CET. We also met with the testing team. Everything that could have been done was done. They explained how, due to the nature of our environment, we cannot effectively perform integration testing on the CET based service. And I know you don't want us messing around with an application that is already in production. Testing as much integration as we could, given our environment, has always proved more than adequate before. Coupled with our enhanced support for the first 30 days after launch, it has always proved more than adequate."

"That was then. This is now, and now is different, as you should have realized by the number of issues we've been having. That's why Jessica brought me here … because of my experience." Ricardo leaned across the desk and jabbed a finger at me as he spoke. "People don't realize that there can be more work required when you put your application out in some kind of Cloud arrangement, than when you keep it completely in-house. They think all they have to do is give the applications to a provider, send a monthly check, then sit back and watch the revenues roll up; that they don't need so many IT people any more, but they're wrong. Clouds add a tremendous amount of complexity to IT's obligations and activities. And they require enhanced coordination between the business, technical and financial teams. Remember that Clouds are just tools. They are not solutions by themselves."

By the tone in his voice, I could tell Ricardo was definitely not interested in a debate about the correctness of what I'd done, or the feasibility of what he was suggesting. "Please help me, then. What should I have been doing that I am not doing"? I asked.

"Aside from the things I just mentioned, you need to manage the operations of Lee's company as if they were part of our company. They are an extension of our IT team.

Anyone who is providing services, whether internal or external, needs to have someone who will look at their claims with a critical eye. You don't have to be negative, but you do have to verify, in some way, what they are saying makes sense. Sure, their data looks fine, but is it too fine? Maybe it's my fault for assuming, based on your background, that you have the maturity and experience to manage this relationship. I just have to say, I am very disappointed you haven't done better."

I had promised Sherm that I wouldn't reveal him as the source of what he'd told me. For a moment I thought how great it would be if I could pin it on Lee. That would be some payback for sure. But since I couldn't be sure where Lee had been and when, much less if he even had the technical knowledge to explain things, it would be easy for someone to catch it as a lie. And that would not be good. Maybe I just needed to make it anonymous.

"I did speak to a friend of mine whose company has been using vendor supplied Cloud components a lot. Without giving him any specifics, I asked his opinion, and he was really surprised that we were looking at capacity and not availability. He said they don't even look at capacity anymore, that the primary driver of their business partners is availability – like having an expensive car that can go 160mph is not useful if the keys are locked inside. They feel that availability of a service identifies its readiness to be used, while capacity of a service establishes the limits of how much can be used."

"Capacity … availability, call it whatever you want. You still have the lead from our company to make this work … to make CET capable of bringing home the revenue we need. Do you realize that your failure with this directly impacts the livelihoods of many employees and stockholders? Don't you feel any sense of obligation to them"?

Ricardo began making a list on a sheet of paper. I could see how upset he was, by watching how hard he was pressing down on the pen. I thought he would rip right through it. Jessica must have really let him have it. Or maybe it was Preston. Those marketing and sales people really knew how to chew people up when it was needed.

"Let me step back a little," said Ricardo. "Do you know why managing our capacity is so important to the success of CET ... why we made that so important during our negotiations with Lee's company"?

I shook my head. "I wasn't part of the planning or execution of those negotiations."

"Because it was clear that given the requirements of our business partners that without the high accessibility and elasticity of different types of Cloud configurations, we would never be able to get CET to deliver what was needed. What metrics and KPIs do you collect and measure independent of what Lee's company gives you"?

"The capacity management team uses best practice capacity metrics ... things like response time, usage trends for our network, impacts on our infrastructure, business partner activity, time in queue, number and length of outages ... things that are important to our business partners," I said. I knew it was a pretty good list because Sean had helped me work it out, and he had a good gut sense of what would be important to users.

Ricardo shook his head. "Those have very little to do with our issues. How did you know that was what our users would want? Did you speak with them"?

"Well, no … not really. But it is kind of obvious to me that these would be important to users. Who wouldn't want to reduce the time they spent waiting, and how fast the application performed. Besides, it's best practice and users just aren't smart enough to know what needs to be watched. Not to mention that we needed to work within the terms of the contract in place."

Ricardo sat back in his chair. His face was getting flushed. It seemed like the more I spoke, the more frustrated and angrier he got. With each word I was digging myself deeper into a hole.

Ricardo held up his tablet and waved it at me, pointing to a page full of text on the screen. I couldn't read it but that much text probably wasn't a note of congratulations.

"This is a copy of an e-mail from Lee to Jessica, complaining about your lack of support and several attempts you've made to undermine our business relationship." Ricardo set the tablet down. "These are very serious charges," he said.

"Let me propose that …"

Ricardo cut me off. "No, it is apparent to me that you cannot self-direct your work. When I give you the opportunity to show us what you can do … how you can act like a professional and get the job done … you become a loose cannon. Your actions threaten a critical business relationship and the company's financial health. Perhaps I am being too lenient, but I don't want to have to terminate you without giving you a chance to succeed. Do you want to leave the company"?

Not again. Now Ricardo was going to put me on a performance improvement plan. Lee was going to get me fired, and to demonstrate how good he was at manipulating people, he was going to have Ricardo do it for him.

"No, not at all. If you want to set up a plan ..."

He cut me off again. "No, I'm not going to put you on a PIP. The time for that is long gone. I am going to be very directive in terms of what you need to do for me, and by when. Understand that these are basic things that a person of your grade and experience should be able to handle, without intervention by your manager."

Ricardo then laid out a series of people he wanted me to meet with, and a list of questions about capacity and the CET application that he wanted answered. I took detailed notes. I was down to my last chance. If I messed this up, Lee would win, and I was not going to allow that.

"And let me be perfectly clear on this, so there can be no room for misunderstanding," he said. "If you fail to meet with these people, obtain the necessary information, or provide a briefing for me in one week's time ... for any reason ... your work will be immediately terminated. Do you understand"?

I nodded.

He said, "That's not enough, I want to hear you explain to me what you are going to do, by when, and the consequences of non-performance."

I parroted back his words as best I could, based on my notes and my memory.

9: Just Sit There and Take It

Ricardo nodded and said, "Fine. Now go get busy. I have my work to do. You had better go do yours."

Tips that would have helped Chris

1. If you are involved with someone who is being deceptive and less than transparent, it can be easy to fall into the same behavior, as a way to respond to them. This is not a good choice. First, it detracts from time you should be spending on moving your project forward. Second, it exposes you to negative consequences if it is discovered. And third, they are probably better at using their approach than yours. By sticking with your values and your company's culture, you make it harder for them to act that way.

2. When leaders and managers are upset with you, whether justifiable or not, trying to argue with them that their perceptions are incorrect, is not a wise course. Take their feedback. Make sure there is clarity and agreement on your next steps and focus on your project.

3. You may find sometimes that leaders or managers are ignorant of availability and capacity implications or needs. While that needs to be corrected, it is not as bad as them having completely incorrect understandings of what they are and how they work. Pick the right time to educate them. Don't embarrass them, and let it become their idea … their realization, not yours. You will have much more success changing their minds.

CHAPTER 10: ONCE MORE UNTO THE BREACH, MY FRIEND?

Early the next morning I walked up to Sean's cube. I stood in the entrance and said, "Sean, I need your help." It was the simplest, most direct way I could think of to get his assistance, with a minimum of sarcasm. When it came to people, Sean was often a real jerk. But when it came to the company's IT operations, he was the one person you always wanted on your side. He'd forgotten more than most people would ever know. And today I needed all of that knowledge.

Sean looked up from his desk and with a big grin said, "Well, that's the first time I've heard you say that ... today"!

He seemed to have recovered from our talk with Sherm. It was reassuring to hear his good old sarcastic tone. I hadn't slept much last night. I kept going over our meeting with Sherm, but the more I did, the more it upset me. Lee was doing it again and that was wrong on so many levels.

I sat down across the desk from Sean and said, "I need to find out if what Sherm told us is true. I want to confront Keshav. I need you to go along to make sure he doesn't give me a bunch of nonsense. You know the technical details better than I do."

"What were you planning to do"? asked Sean. "Were you going to simply walk into his office ... a director's office, and accuse him of unethical behavior that was against the best interests of the company, its stockholders, its customers, and its employees? What do you expect to happen then? If it were true, would you expect Keshav to simply confess to you? And if it weren't true, what do you expect he would do"?

"I don't know. I probably didn't think this out very much. But we can't let this continue."

"So let's do the right thing first, not to mention the thing that will prevent you from getting summarily fired," said Sean, as he pulled a set of charts out and onto the desk. "I ran some reports based on serviceability, reliability and availability of CET. Take a look and let's see if that really is the issue."

As Sean took me through the charts, they showed a completely different story from what Lee's presentations had said. It appeared that once CET failed anywhere, there were subsequently cascades of failures that ultimately took down the entire application faster than the failed pieces could be restored. Restoration seemed to take a very long time, reflecting an awkward and time-consuming process, and to make matters worse, once there had been a broad failure, CET remained unstable for quite a while after it was restored and was prone to subsequent failures, with little notice.

"It's pretty clear we need to do a better job of availability management," I said.

"That's something you need to design it in," said Sean.

"And that is where I need your help," I said. "I've got to have a heart to heart with Keshav about CET. And I know they respect you, your knowledge, and your experience. I want to know how much they considered availability when designing and testing CET."

10: Once More Unto the Breach, My Friend?

"Whereas they think you are a piece of old gum stuck to the bottom of their shoe," said Sean, and with a laugh added, "And they are probably right. Besides, Ricardo gave you fair warning that your performance was a whole lot worse. You know what that means." Sean drew his index finger across his throat.

"How do you know that? You weren't in the room with Ricardo and me."

"True, but I also got a phone call from Lee a couple of days ago. You do remember Lee, don't you"?

I scowled at Sean, and wondered how well he knew Lee, and what kind of relationship they had. Sean knew all about my history with Lee, and how he had lied to get me onto a performance improvement plan so he would keep me in line, and to create fear in others that he might do the same to them. Were Sean and Lee of similar minds, or was it more adversarial, like Lee was with me? I'd always considered Sean to be on my side. Once you cut through the sarcasm, we seemed to be aligned on almost everything. More practically, Sean hadn't said anything about this when he talked to Sherm and me. I wondered how much else may have been withheld, and what he was going to share back with Lee. And in the worst case, was he also secretly working with Lee?

"What did my 'friend' want"? I asked.

"Actually, he was asking about you … in an indirect way. He wanted to know who I thought was the best person here to manage the relationship between our company and his company. He was asking if there was someone who could be quickly put in place if you were to move on to another assignment somewhere. He was indirectly offering the role to me, I think. I made sure he understood I was not interested. Can you imagine ... talk about a career ending role. You're the only one dumb enough to take those kinds of jobs. Well, I guess you know that by now."

Sometimes Sean's total lack of impulse control was annoying, but occasionally, it could be of real value ... and this was one of those times. He had just confirmed what I'd expected; that Lee had been setting me up to be the victim, so he could walk away looking like the concerned, yet heroic, partner, who was willing to make the tough decisions.

"But how did you know Ricardo and I talked about ..."?

"I had breakfast with Jessica yesterday morning. She invited me so she could get my input on some things ... and one of those was ... you. It was pretty clear to me, based on what I've seen before, that someone was going to have what they euphemistically refer to as a 'difficult conversation' with you yesterday and I assumed it would be your manager."

Part of me wanted to laugh. I couldn't believe the amount of management time that was being spent talking about me behind my back. It would have been so much simpler and quicker if we'd all just sat down in a room and talked about it. But then it would look like management wasn't sure what to do and leadership definitely did not like looking any way except decisive.

As we headed to Keshav's office, Sean said, "Remember, no accusations. We are going there just to collect facts. Everything needs to be fact-based. If you start accusing a director of what you're thinking, without any evidence, I doubt even I can help."

10: Once More Unto the Breach, My Friend?

When Sean and I arrived for the meeting, Keshav seemed engrossed in the two screens on his desk, streaming what appeared to be some kind of performance charts. I reached out to knock, but Sean shook his head and simply walked in. I sat down in one of the office chairs across the desk from Keshav, while Sean walked around behind the desk and bent over, lowering his head down to the same height as Keshav's and stared at the screen.

After a moment, Sean reached out, tapped the screen with his finger, and said, "I was told this rig would be able to tell me the meaning of life."

Keshav looked up and gave Sean a shove away from the screen. "The meaning of life is that if you want to continue living, you won't disturb me when I'm working."

"Okay," said Sean. "We'll wait." Sean reached over Keshav's head and grabbed a couple of his prized tech toys from the shelf. He walked back around to where I was and after sitting down, offered one to me. "Want a toy to play with until Keshav, the great and powerful, is ready to give us an audience"?

Keshav stopped what he was doing, turned around in his chair, and snatched the toys from Sean's hands. "Look, everyone isn't even here yet. While you may not have anything else to do, those of us in development are extremely busy, and until Ricardo gets here, I'm going to keep working."

"Ricardo"? asked Sean. "You're expecting Ricardo? Oh, no. It's just the two of us. Ricardo had a conflict come up. He was sure you would understand."

Keshav scowled. "I wish he had let me know. We could have rescheduled our meeting."

I tried not to smile. I had asked Ricardo to set the meeting up under his name, even though he had no plans to attend. It was a deception, but one which guaranteed Keshav would accept the meeting.

Keshav looked directly at Sean. "And if I had realized you would be here, I wouldn't have accepted the meeting invite, even if it were from Jessica herself. You are just as irritating and tiresome now as you were when I worked for you so long ago."

Sean laughed out loud. "But don't you even want to thank me for hiring you? I still don't know if you were a good hire or not. Maybe I was a little hungover from the night before and you wore me down."

Keshav rolled his eyes and said, "Let's get started. The sooner we start, the sooner I can get you out of here and get my space back."

We never even got through the first question I had. The interaction between Keshav and Sean was like watching a couple of genius level kids try to outdo each other. In other circumstances it might have been interesting for a few moments, but today and here … not at all. I didn't have the time for it.

When it got to the point where I couldn't take it anymore, I interrupted them and said to Keshav, "Why didn't you consider availability in your design? Why didn't you ensure CET's availability would meet our service commitments? It's in the company's best interest and that makes it part of your job. Do you feel your team's design met that standard"?

Out of the corner of my eye, I caught Sean wince as I spoke. Yes, he had warned me that publicly putting it too directly to Keshav would be perceived as an assault on his integrity and provoke immediate pushback ... from a person who was several grades higher in the organization.

Keshav sat silently, glaring at me. His faced was flushed. After what seemed like hours, he closed the material displayed on his desk and said, "This meeting is over. Goodbye." He then turned his chair around and sitting with his back to us, he began to work on his computers.

Sean waved me out of the office and said, "Chris, why don't you go ahead. I want to stay and have a couple of words with Keshav in private. I'll catch up with you later."

I was nearly back to my cube when Sean came around the corner.

"I hope you have enjoyed your tenure at the company," he said. This time there was no undercurrent of humor to his words. "If I know Keshav ... and I do. You are now going to receive some serious, corrective coaching by your boss and his boss. Frankly, I'd do the same thing in his position."

"But we already know he was acting unethically and should not be allowed to stay. He's got to be getting something from Lee in return. We know the things Keshav did. Sherm told us in no uncertain terms."

Sean shook his head. "After talking with Keshav, I'm not so sure anymore. I think that perhaps Sherm was either confused ... or maybe even lying. I think you may have just accused an innocent person of some very ugly actions."

I thought about Sean's sudden change of perspective. I was sure Sherm was being truthful. He wasn't smart enough, or manipulative enough, to lie about it. I know what Lee had done to me, and I could see him doing it to Sherm. I couldn't help Sherm, but I could understand how reasonable his motivation could be. But if Sherm were telling the truth about Keshav, why had Sean so suddenly decided otherwise. Sean had seen what Lee did to me. He knew the way Lee worked. It didn't make sense for Sean to flip like that.

Then I remembered that implication that Sean knew Sherm … that they had talked before. But since Sherm had only recently been assigned to this project, how could they have talked about it before it began? Unless Lee had also promised Sean his job would be retained after a mass IT layoff. He fit the profile. He had a broad knowledge of the entire infrastructure, knew everyone on the business side, and most importantly, had the trust and ear of senior leadership.

My heart sank. Was Sean working for Lee too?

Tips that would have helped Chris

1. There will be occasions where you receive excellent advice from trusted friends and yet you still ignore it. There can be serious consequences as a result of it. It's a mistake. Everyone makes them. Don't ignore it. Don't deny it. Learn from it and move on.

2. When you are trying to get your project in place, you may uncover a tiny bit of data that tends to point to a particular solution. A common tendency is to jump on it, treat it as a fact and act as if it were correct. Many times you will go down a false path. One point does not make a line. Continue to gather additional bits of data for as long as prudent. If you want to change people's behavior, it is much easier if you have an unquestionable array of facts, rather than a single data point.

3. If you have ever been the victim of corporate intrigue, you will probably see plots and schemers around every corner. That's your defenses talking. Ignore them for a while. Work extra hard to assume good intent. It will free up more time for your project and make people more receptive to the behaviors you want them to adopt.

CHAPTER 11: REPRIMAND BY REMOTE CONTROL

When I walked into his office, Ricardo didn't even look up. He kept working on his computer in silence. When he finally stopped typing, he cleared the screen and said to me, "How is the CET capacity project going? Have you figured out how to stop these outages? Or have you made another decision"?

"It is coming along. One of the things we've uncovered is that it truly does need to be focused on availability, not capacity."

Ricardo shook his head. "Chris, I've already told you, I don't care what you call it, I just want it fixed. Clearly, you are stuck in trying to slap a name onto it, instead of getting down to fixing it. Move on. Get it fixed. The business wants confidence we will meet our service level commitments to them. They don't care about why it breaks. They only want it not to break. Can you at least move on and solve that for me? You don't have a lot of time. Rest assured, I will not move out the deadline. I've already made commitments to my management, and I will not go back on them." Ricardo paused for a few moments then added, "Have you even done the basics like identifying what the expectations are for performance, as laid out in the SLAs? Or do you even know what the underlying products and services are to deliver CET"?

"Not in a form I'd care to present to you today," I said, waving a pile of papers at Ricardo. "But I can have it summarized in an executive form for you tomorrow. I don't want to waste your time going through all my detailed notes." I lied and I wasn't happy about it. I had spent very little time on availability, but if I continued to try and explain that we had only just concluded that the issue was availability, not capacity, he would go crazy.

Ricardo scowled and shook his head. "That's what I thought." He paused for a moment and added, "I want an update of your progress tomorrow and a forecast of what is left to do."

I nodded, and as I started collecting my material said, "No problem. You've got it. Is there anything else"? Ricardo looked seriously unhappy and I was hoping I could get away with just a rush presentation assignment.

"Yes, there is. It's why I set up this meeting," said Ricardo. "I have been informed that you have accused a long-term employee, with a solid work history, of unethical actions related to CET, which, if true, would be grounds for immediate termination of this individual. And that you confronted this person with these accusations in the presence of other employees. Is this true"?

"Which person are you talking about"? I asked.

"Do you do this so often that there is a list of possible individuals? Are you serious"?

I shook my head. "No, it's just that I want to understand what I said that might have been incorrectly construed as an accusation. I am trying to drive this work to a rapid conclusion. And I know that when I am trying to quickly bring a project to closure, I can be terse and very direct. Someone who was not accustomed to plain-spoken dialogue might misconstrue dialogue for an accusation."

Ricardo seemed to ponder that for a moment, then added, "I might be willing to accept that kind of mistake by you were there only one person who perceived it. However, there were witnesses to your behavior and they all independently came away with the same perception of your intent. Moreover, when I reviewed your file and read the notes in it, I saw a disturbing tendency to throw other people under the bus ... to blame them ... for any of your failures or inability to meet deadlines. Your permanent record showed a pattern of behavior consistent with the complaints brought against you."

"You can't believe what is in my file. It's full of lies manufactured by Lee, my prior manager, to justify putting me on a performance improvement program. None of it is true ..."

Ricardo cut me off. "This is exactly what I mean, Chris. You've done something inappropriate and rather than take ownership of your error, you try to blame it on someone else. We all make mistakes. If we never make a mistake, we will never learn. The only way you get better is to acknowledge your mistakes, own them, and work to make them not happen again. The worst thing you can do is to deny them, because then you will repeat them over and over again."

"But that is not what is happening here ..."

"Chris, I've had multiple complaints ... and I might add, so has Jessica ... from both inside and outside the company. This is just another. It cannot continue."

I didn't listen to the rest of what Ricardo was saying. Outside the company could only come from one person – Lee. And if he complained, then it was proof Keshav was involved ... and Sean? It sure looked like it. They must have been the ones from inside. The outside person could only have been Lee. My world of trusted associates was shrinking. Except for Sherm, who worked for the outsourcer, I was on my own.

There was a knock at the door and before Ricardo could say anything, Jessica stuck her head through the partially open door.

"Hi Ricardo. Oh, I see that Chris is here. That's perfect. May we come and sit in for a moment"?

Ricardo nodded, the door opened wide and in walked Jessica and Lee, who closed the door after them. They sat down on either side of me.

"Hi Lee," said Ricardo. "How are you feeling now"?

Lee sat back in the chair, crossing his legs as he did. He smoothed the lapels on his suit's jacket and brushed the legs in his pants as if he were smoothing out wrinkles, but of course, there were none.

He was always vastly overdressed for our company, but by now I was convinced that he wore an expensive suit everywhere. Probably even to the gym. In fact, I was beginning to doubt anyone had ever seen him less than immaculately dressed.

Lee sat quiet for a moment, his eyes almost closed, as if he were pondering some weighty matter. Finally, after everyone else was settled and the room was quiet, he opened his eyes, looked at Ricardo and said, "I'm fine, Ricardo. Thank you for taking the time to respond to my concerns. Between your assurances and those of Jessica, I think there is no permanent damage done." He turned to

Jessica and said, "As I was explaining to Jessica ... and she agreed ... some people can handle pressure to deliver critical projects and others cannot." Lee turned and looked directly at me. He wore that annoying smirk as he said, "Unfortunately, the only way to find that out is to give them the opportunity to succeed and see if they take advantage of it. That's what I've been doing with Sherman. Unfortunately, I have not been as successful with him as I would have liked. Then again, anyone can make a genius look smart; the real task of management is to make weak players better."

"I would definitely agree," said Jessica with a smile. "I am double booked right now, so I'll leave you all to your meeting. Thanks again, Lee."

Lee waited until she was gone, then said, "Ricardo, I'm more than willing to simply write this off as people struggling to cope with the pressure to deliver." Lee interlocked his fingers on his lap and said, "Not all of us are meant to deal with life in the fast lane, but sometimes we can coach them in how to do their best within their capabilities."

I waved my hands at Ricardo. "Wait a minute. If you have issues with my performance, that's fine. Let's have that discussion. But it should be done one on one, in a confidential way that's respectful to the employee but still addresses the issues." That I knew was straight out of the company handbook. I knew because Lee had read it to me last time. "Lee is not an employee of this company. He is an employee of a third party vendor. He should not be part of this discussion."

Lee shook his head and said, "Ricardo, I know that you, Jessica and I had already talked about this, so I will defer to your explanation to Chris."

"Thanks, Lee," said Ricardo.

I couldn't believe it. Here was a third party employee giving my manager permission to be a manager, and my manager thanked him for it. I couldn't think of a thing to say.

Ricardo stared at me. "Lee and his company are not a typical third party vendor. They are extensions of our company. We are dependent on them for our success. He is subject to the same confidentiality rules as any employee. Furthermore, he is a former employee of our company and your former manager, so he has some special insight into you, your motivations and how best to coach you for better success in the future. As your manager I value his input, as does the rest of the leadership team."

Just as Ricardo was completing his justification of Lee's involvement, the sound of Orff's, O Fortuna from Carmina Burana pulsed from inside Lee's jacket. Lee smiled and pulled out his phone. He turned away from us and spoke quietly. Muting his phone, he said, "Please excuse me. I need to attend another meeting with Sherman. Once again he ignored my coaching and now finds himself in over his head. I'm not sure I can, or want, to keep saving him like this. Not everyone is worth saving, you know."

Lee held the phone away, and speaking to Ricardo and me, said, "Hopefully, the two of you can work together to get things back on track." Without waiting for our response, he stood up and still talking on the phone walked out of Ricardo's office.

11: Reprimand by Remote Control

I was stunned for a moment. Somehow, Lee had convinced my management that he was right, and I was just a sub-standard employee eager to blame others for my shortcomings. And the worst part was he had done it using the same set of lies he'd fabricated to justify putting me on a performance improvement plan when he was my manager.

Thankfully, Ricardo broke the silence. "What can I expect to see from you tomorrow, Chris"?

The only way I was going to get this turned around was to be assertive about what needed to be done and how we were going to do it. Fortunately, Sherm had come to my aid and explained to me what we should have and what Lee's company should be doing.

"It's more than just tomorrow," I said. "Sure, I can give you a list of things that will be delivered, but unless it is part of a larger plan that ensures we get everything we need, we're always going to be fighting fires. Let's not make the same mistake they made when they designed CET and do it piecemeal, let's build a larger plan and break out what gets done when."

I stood up and walked over to Ricardo's white board, picked up a marker and started to draw.

I drew two clusters of boxes to represent the underlying products and services necessary to deliver the CET service. One group I labeled as our responsibility and the other as belonging to Lee's company. I circled the two groups and drew a line from there to another box labeled as service delivery. It had another box coming off it labeled customer satisfaction and I drew a connection labeled feedback from there back to the areas Lee's company and our company owned.

"This is what we want to manage. But we've got to stop calling it capacity. It is availability."

"Semantics," said Ricardo.

"No," I said. "You're thinking about performance. You need to manage both capacity and availability in order to ensure performance. Think of availability as required for the customer to use the service, and capacity as how much of the service the customer can use. Availability of the service is the core of customer satisfaction. We can't succeed without it. The good news is that a properly designed service can deliver service and customer satisfaction, even if things go wrong. But you have to make that part of the design. You can't paste it on at the end by bringing in third party resources, like you can with capacity."

"If you are suggesting we do not have that built into the design, doesn't that mean we have a risk that cannot be mitigated"? asked Ricardo.

"I'm suggesting that we need to answer some fundamental questions first, and so far I haven't seen any attempts to do that. Do we know what level of availability is acceptable to our customers"?

Ricardo chuckled, "That's easy, 100%."

"That's always the answer. What we never did was help them understand that just as having infinite capacity for growth instantly available has a material incremental cost, so complete and constant availability has a material cost. It's like with disaster recovery. Customers want restoration during an event that's so fast they don't even notice it, and have zero risk of losing even a single keystroke of data. But when you work closely with them and they understand that that level of service costs several orders of magnitude more than 90% within 30 minutes and 100% with 72 hours, their answer changes dramatically. It is a difficult conversation that must be had for the sake of the company."

As I continued, I realized that Ricardo was really engaged. He liked what we were doing. Maybe this is what he had been looking for all along – sleeves rolled up, brainstorming solutions with me, learning what I'd discovered and knew. Maybe my biggest mistake had been not figuring out what form of interaction was acceptable to him ... what would create managerial satisfaction.

I just hoped that this would improve his opinion of me. Because if it didn't, I knew I wouldn't even get the formality of a performance improvement plan, I'd simply be out of here.

Tips that would have helped Chris

1. Understand the style of interaction with your boss. Some have a very formal style. They want written reports for them to review in private. Others want to roll up their sleeves and brainstorm with you. They want to be part of the solution discovery. This will greatly improve your ability to communicate effectively with them and nudge them into different behavior patterns. The hard part is, most people are a situational mix of styles. Try to become adept at assessing, on the fly, the best way to interact with someone. Practise it all the time.

2. Another leader's opinion of you and your work may carry more weight with some bosses than what you actually do. This is unfortunate and often indicates a manager who is not very involved in what you are doing. The best way to countermand this is to consistently demonstrate to your manager the quality and effectiveness of the work you are doing. It needs to be done subtlety, perhaps starting with just informational awareness of things you are accomplishing that they may not be immediately aware of. You can build it into a more regular and detailed sharing as they become accustomed to it. You see a similar phenomenon when leadership gives more weight to a consultant's recommendation than one from their own staff, even though they are the same. This behavior is based on several misconceptions. Two examples are: The "Bigger Fool" theory – if someone else paid for it then it must be valuable and you are saving by listening to it; The "Price Equals Value" theory – where if you pay a lot for it, it must be better.

3. It is important that your end to end services are designed in such a way that small failures in individual components do not materially impact the end to end service delivered to the customer. Ideally, that end to end service needs to be resilient, robust and have some level of self-healing or alternate pathways available.

CHAPTER 12: SUCCESS FEELS GOOD

I was still soaring from the meeting I'd had with Ricardo. It had been a long time since I'd had such a positive discussion with any leader at this company ... a real dialogue where I was adding value ... advancing the state of the organization. Given that success, it seemed like a great time to go back to Keshav and perhaps share my knowledge with him. `

I'd thought about bringing Sherm along. After all, he was the source of my education and he was our supplier partner. It only made sense. But I was so full of confidence and really wanted to see if Keshav truly was working with Lee, and I didn't want to put Sherm at any more risk than I already had. He'd done the right thing and while people sometimes got punished for doing what was right, I was not going to be a part of that.

Keshav's office was empty when I arrived, but in a bit of luck, just as I was about to leave, he came walking down the corridor.

"I don't think we have a meeting right now," said Keshav. "In fact, I'm sure of it, so why are you here"?

I decided to take a different approach from the last time.

"I was concerned that in my desire to get to a solution, my questions came across as inappropriate. My apologies for that. I would like the opportunity to ask you a few other questions in a much more temperate manner."

"Keep talking," said Keshav.

"After our last talk, I was left with a number of questions, but I still have to present the results to my leaders. I know we only touched the surface about application development, but you are clearly the expert. I trust your assessment of the situation. If you could find a few minutes to help clear up some of the larger gaps in my knowledge, I would be very grateful."

Like Sean had told me once, you've got to give trust in order to get trust. I needed to confirm what Sean had talked about and get some inkling of whether Keshav really had aligned himself with Lee against the interest of the company. That meant I needed to trust Keshav ... or at least act like I trusted him ... for now.

Keshav sighed and said, "Okay, come on in. This is planned as open office time for my team. But if one of my staff needs me, then our meeting is over. Make no mistake. Any of them comes before you."

It seemed that Keshav had a strong sense of loyalty, or at least professed one.

As we sat down, I decided it would be a better approach to try and establish a personal connection with Keshav, before digging into the work issues.

"When I look around your office," I said, "I get the impression you've worked here a really long time."

Keshav nodded, "I was one of the earlier hires. Then Sean hired me on right after the company went public and they finally had some cash. It took them a number of years to get to that point. It was a good thing, too. Sean had been scraping along for so long that he was nearly a burn-out case by then."

"Wow. So what was it like to have him as your manager? He must have been able to educate you on a lot of things."

Keshav sniffed. "Not about design, that's for sure. I've got a lot more education than he does, more training and more experience in design. That's why he hired me ... because I'm a lot smarter than him. At least that was one thing he did right."

"What do you mean"? I asked.

"Look, he was still a new manager. Most of the work he'd done before I got here, he did by himself. He didn't have a lot of experience as a manager. He made a lot of mistakes. But to his credit, he learned from them and one of the lessons he eventually learned was that he didn't like managing people. He loved to mentor and coach them, but he hated managing them. That's why he has no direct reports now and hasn't had any for quite a few years. He had the intelligence and courage to stand up and admit to everyone what his strengths were and what his weaknesses were."

"That's hard to imagine. He seems so relaxed today ... so confident and in command. Nothing seems to bother him."

"He's very different now than he was back then. He is still just as annoying as always, but he is just one of those technical experts who is best left as a technical expert and not forced into being a manager. It was a hard decision for him. It cost him a huge number of stock options from when the company went public ... more than enough for him to have retired years ago. They were only available to managers, so he had to forfeit them. He was really angry about it at the time, but I think he got over it. I don't think it was fair by the company. That's the kind of treatment that can just eat at you. Fortunately, I think he got over it. At least he had options, even if they did get taken away. People like myself who were hired after the company went public, got nothing, even though we are the ones who made the company what it is. I guess we didn't get any so the executives could have lots for themselves. You know how that works."

"Those are some great insights. If you know something about what people have been through then you can understand their behavior better, especially since anger over unfairness rarely goes completely away. Sometimes it can fester for a long time until it resurfaces."

"An excellent diagnosis, Dr Freud," said Keshav, as he leaned back in his chair. But we're not here to talk about the history of the company or psychoanalyze its employees. What do you want to know"?

"I've been doing some research and I found a lot of agreement that when looking at the availability of an application there are several essential KPIs we should be tracking ... measures we can use to assess the performance of Lee's company ... to make sure we are getting value and supporting our customers. I know you said availability was an infrastructure issue, not a design one, but since you know so much about CET, I wanted your perspective."

"I don't remember if we talked about it when you were last here with Sean."

"We didn't, but since this has been outsourced to Lee's company, I was hoping your experience managing third parties might help us determine the right measures to use. For example, everyone talks about end to end monitoring

.... of actual service delivery being essential when assessing the state of availability."

"That's fine," said Keshav. "Fine provided that you are talking about internal infrastructure. But when you give up all responsibility to a third party, they're not going to provide you with that level of visibility. So you have to measure the results ... measure the outputs in terms of timeliness and quality. It's all you can do. But don't be fooled into thinking that just because outputs are coming through on time, that there are no untoward events or issues inside the third party."

"Why should I care"? I asked. "As long as the service is being delivered on time and on spec, how they do it doesn't matter to me. We're paying for results, not for how they got there."

"That's wrong. Third parties may try to convince you that it's always delivered because of the nature of the Cloud you're working with, or through great response of over allocation of resources. They want you to have that false sense of security because they don't want to have to explain and justify to you how your service is managed or delivered, as long as it is what you contracted for. The less you know, the easier to manage, and more profitable it is for them."

I shook my head. "As long as my customers are getting what they say they need ... on time and with the appropriate functionality ... why should I care about the third party guys? I don't get what you're trying to say. For me, with a third party provider, the service is what's delivered at the end point."

"When I first got out of college," said Keshav. "I went to work for an insurance company. I had a good friend in the claims department and you know what she said to me"?

I resisted the urge to add a flip comment and simply shook my head.

"She told me that the difference between a $1,000 payout and a $100,000 payout in an automobile accident is about three inches. Not knowing what's happening in the third party environment blinds you. You don't know if they barely managed to squeak out the service today, or if it were so easy they all went home early. To make matters worse, by focusing only on whether there is delivery or not, you start looking at availability measures as reactive flags that are addressed if they happen, but then discarded and not viewed in the larger context. You're looking at the 'Yes or No' flags but not the 'How Much' ones."

"Like statistical process control"? I asked.

"I'm impressed. I thought you were like the typical infrastructure knuckle-dragger who occasionally finds their way here without getting lost. You are exactly right. Things break ... things show variation to standard. You can't prevent it. That's why no one ever really operates at the sixth sigma level. I am less afraid of the occasional service failure than I am of service elements that are green but are continually threatening to go red. They virtually guarantee that one day they will go red ... you will have a major service failure, and from your perspective, it will have appeared out of the blue. But in actuality, it will have been signaling a problem for weeks or months. You want to hang on to that availability data and use it to identify trends as part of your continual improvement of the service."

"So when leadership is focused on capacity, they're looking at the wrong thing? Is that what you are saying"? I asked.

"No," said Keshav. "You need them both. Availability is all about how long a service is available to be utilized, but capacity is about how much can be utilized. But leadership seems obsessively focused on how much and not enough on how long."

"Got it," I said.

Keshav poked his finger at me. "Then you must be smarter than our leadership. I tried to explain it to them and they ignored me. They thought they knew more than I did about the subject, even though it's been years ... perhaps even decades ... since some of them have had to actually work day-to-day operational issues. Like a bad case of leadership presbyopia, they can no longer see anything immediate or specific ... only generalized long-term issues. Decisive actions are only good if you are actually qualified to make that decision. That's why you can't blame them too much for the confusion. Capability, by its nature, tends to be more strategic, more long-term focused. Availability tends to be more here and now."

"Is that why they signed the contract we have? I've looked through it all and I don't see requirements for Lee's company to do anything even slightly related to what you've talked about."

Keshav shook his head. "In their ignorant hubris, they created this problem, and from what I've seen, refuse to take accountability for it. They just want people like you to make it work somehow. And that is not fair."

12: Success Feels Good

I left our meeting still wondering if Keshav had acted on his frustrations and joined with Lee. He had plenty of reasons. The question was, had he acted on them?

Tips that would have helped Chris

1. Understand that different people have different views of the company you both work for. They may have a very negative view. If they do, that doesn't mean you need to adopt a similar view in order to facilitate changing their behavior to support your project. You only need to be sympathetic and willing to listen. In most cases that is sufficient.

2. People's frustrations can create a huge barrier to your attempts to change their behavior in support of your project. Different people deal with their frustrations in different ways. Some act them out, others simply want to keep expressing them. You need to help them see how your project will not increase their frustrations and will most likely improve their situation. Much frustration comes from people feeling as if no one treats them properly. Bringing them in as part of the solution can often provide them with proof that you want to help them.

3. When things go right, especially if they haven't for a while, it is important to take a moment and let yourself feel good about it.

CHAPTER 13: NO PLAN SURVIVES CONTACT WITH REALITY

I sat alone in the conference room. I'd reserved it for 30 minutes before the meeting was to begin. I wanted the time to center myself, to get ready. CET was at a critical point and so was I. The business was losing faith in our ability to keep its service available. People were expecting me to produce a solution for them. This was going to be the most important meeting I'd led in front of leadership since I got here. And if it didn't go well ... then it would probably be my last meeting at this company.

I was calm, the calm that comes from being confident ... not the false bravado of someone trying to convince themselves, as well as others. I was calm because I was ready.

The presentation was ready. It was one of the best I had ever prepared. It was laid out in terms that even my leadership could understand. Things were what they would call, "focused," I'd call them "simple minded." I knew my message was right ... it was exactly what we needed to get CET delivering the services our business partners needed.

I'd gotten a good night's sleep. I was ready to present. I knew the material. I'd practiced the presentation for timing, but hadn't done it so many times it would sound stilted. Most importantly, I had taken Ricardo, Jessica and Preston through the material before today; to get their comments, updates and concurrence with what I was saying and proposing. There was nothing here that they would find surprising. They would be looking more for the comments and questions of others at the meeting, than raising their own.

I was a little surprised that Lee was the first person to arrive. While that was not his normal practice ... he preferred to make an entrance when everyone was waiting, he was unmistakable in his foppish sartorial splendor – a hollow suit full of deceit and narcissism.

Looking disappointed that there was no one else there to admire his arrival, he walked over and stood beside me.

"Chris? I hadn't expected to see you at this meeting. I was under the impression that this was going to be a small leadership group from your company." In a sarcastic voice, he added, "And I haven't seen anything about a recent promotion for you to vice president. Did I miss something"?

I nodded. "What? You mean that with all your skill and connections you missed the announcement that I'm the new VP of operations"? I figured that since the meeting hadn't started yet, a little verbal tete-a-tete fun was within the bounds of propriety. Normally, with just the two of us here, I'd not be worried, knowing that it would be his word against mine. But given how much leadership seemed to love Lee, I couldn't count on that.

"Very good, Chris. So you can think on your feet after all." Lee sat down and arranged himself in the chair beside me, then leaned over ... directly into my personal space and too close for my comfort to where his apparently fresh application of too much cologne smelled overwhelming. It was a waste of Serge Lutens Borneo 1834. I felt intimidated by his actions, but that was probably the desired result. I swore to myself I would not let it show.

I said to Lee, "I'm surprised Sherm isn't following along behind you, carrying all your documents and notes."

"Ah yes, Sherman. I'm surprised you would even ask such a question after the discussion the two of you had in that coffee shop. You ought to know me well enough by now that I value loyalty very highly and his seeking you out and having that discussion was definitely disloyal ... wouldn't you agree"? said Lee.

I was dumb-struck. How could he know about that? I'd said nothing about it. "What do you mean"? I blurted out.

Lee shook his head. "Don't ever play poker, Chris. You are as open as a book with large print type. I'll be direct for your benefit. Sherman is no longer around. Did he tell you he was on a performance improvement plan? Well, he's now moved on to other challenges. He is experiencing the consequences of his actions."

I couldn't believe it. Lee had fired Sherm because he told me about the ethical lapses during the negotiations of the contract. And the way Lee seemed to almost take joy in the firing, made me even madder. He looked at it like a game.

Before I could say anything more, the room began to fill up with attendees. Lee stood up and switched to a seat at the head of the table, as he always liked to do. Besides, I didn't think he wanted to be seen near me, since I couldn't do anything for him, or make him look more important.

Ricardo, Jessica, Preston, and all of the other key leaders, were present at the table. Behind them, up against the walls, sat their supporting players ... the people who had the knowledge, and could quickly provide key points of clarification to their own leader, if needed. They were necessary so that the leaders would always look like they knew more and were in command. At this company, for a senior leader to seem uninformed or not in command, was just as bad as a regular employee being put on a performance improvement plan.

Three people were noticeable by their absence. Sherm was gone ... thanks to Lee. Keshav was also missing. Perhaps my message had gotten through and actions were being taken. That made me feel a little better ... like leaders were actually trusting my word. It's amazing how much trust builds your confidence.

Once everyone settled down, I turned on the large LCD screen on one wall and began to explain the issue and our recommendations.

"I will not be revisiting the decision to host CET with a third party Cloud. That does not appear to be the cause of the issues we have been having. IT organizations natively focus on processing tangible items related to events or requests. That's things like incidents, changes, problems, and the like. We do those very well. However, resolving our current challenge requires a focus on processing items that focus on intangible attributes. In our case, those are availability and capacity. Don't think they are less important just because they focus on intangibles. In fact, success in activities processing tangible items is dependent on a strong availability process. Availability is at the heart of customer satisfaction. But it isn't easy to manage. It requires an end to end understanding of how any service supports the customer and the infrastructure components required to deliver it. And that requires a good grasp of capacity for the service."

I switched to an image chart of some key ITSM related processes. "The easy way to think about them is that availability is whether or not something is available to be utilized, and capacity is how much of it can be utilized. And that's where our challenge is."

Preston interrupted me.

"Wait a minute, Chris. How can we understand all the infrastructure components our Cloud provider ... in this case, Lee's company ... is providing? We can know when we spec'd out, but under the contract, they aren't responsible for matching it. All they are responsible for is making CET available via a Cloud environment ... I forget which kind ... public, private, hybrid, super double secret ..."

A few people chuckled at Preston's idea of a super double secret Cloud.

"Laugh if you want," he said in good humor. "But the fact remains that Lee's company is on the hook for only a couple of things ... making CET available via their Cloud environments ... ensuring there is adequate capacity to handle the volumes we predicted ... providing first-level response, and reporting to us on their performance. So once we turn it over to them, it shouldn't be our problem. Isn't that right"?

Lee nodded and said, "My company will manage everything we've signed up for. We'll take care of those for you, so they are not your problem. You can count on that. I give you my word."

I shook my head. "Those are true statements. But you must remember to separate out Cloud marketing from the reality. People often have an incorrect belief that the elasticity and scalability of Clouds virtually eliminates the need for capacity management. Adding Cloud elements actually adds complexity and requires a combination of business, financial, and technical expertise. Don't forget that Clouds are really just tools ... great tools ... but still just tools."

"If Lee's company is providing everything they should, then why is Preston coming to me much too often crying about not being able to make his numbers for the year because CET is down too often"? asked Jonah. "If Lee's company is delivering as they should but we still have disruptions, does that mean our IT team is not capable of working this way ... that we cannot explore any business models besides the one we have"?

Lee added, "I'm sure you understand that our processes are proprietary and it would be inappropriate, and outside the boundaries of our contractual relationship for our SMEs, to share anything about our methods or techniques with others, whether it covered anything from design to operations."

"It goes beyond that," I said. "CET is an amazingly complex application ... perhaps too complex for us to really measure its capacity needs and utilization on an end to end basis. Just as with testing something so complicated, sometimes the best you can do is evaluate the individual functional components in it. The only hint of positive news there is that the approach is very much aligned with the war room model IT uses for responding to requests and incidents."

I pulled up the next slide, the one on availability. "While we can't manage capacity the way we would if everything were in-house, we can, and will, hold Lee's company accountable for ensuring the capacity cushion identified in the contract is always present."

"No problem," said Lee. "My company has your back. And as long as the forecasts we get from Preston's teams are close to reality, it should not be an issue."

Jonah spoke up. "Then what is causing these disruptions? If Lee's company is meeting their obligations and our IT team is handling their end ..." he looked over at Preston. "And Preston's forecasts are good, then what button is left for us to push to make sure the service is available for him to use"?

"You've perfectly identified the issue and pointed to the solution," I said. "The challenge is availability, not capacity."

"Now you're throwing semantics at us," said Jonah. "How can we possibly manage that any better if it's in a Cloud somewhere?"

"We can measure and track availability of the service that comes out of the Cloud Lee's company provides. Key measures like the number and duration of disruptions, the time from restoration to next disruption, the time between disruptions, the time to restore from a disruption. There are a number of measures we can use to manage availability. Untoward things will happen, no matter what we do. What we want to manage is collection of information, to let us know before something becomes an issue, and either fix it beforehand, or else supplement the design with redundancies sufficient to absorb those types of shocks, without diminishing the service provided to support our revenue and business goals."

Lee smiled and spoke directly to Jonah. "Those are important things, but I would like to point out they are services from my company that you elected not to include in our contractual arrangement and therefore are not reflected in our pricing," said Lee. "However, as your partner we would be happy to sit down with you and assess what additional efforts my company could perform for you, to ensure we meet your determination of need."

"Sure ... we can meet on that," said Jonah. He then turned back to Preston and Jessica. "But why wasn't this all covered when you built this contract with Lee's company? Why wasn't it part of the contract I signed"?

I took a risk and did what I think Sean would have done were he in my place, but in my own style. I was not going to throw anyone under the bus ... I was not Lee. I wanted this to stay productive and not become vindictive.

"That's an excellent question," I said. "And if Jessica and Preston don't object, I'd like to answer it for you." Without giving either Jessica or Preston a chance to speak, I moved forward, "The contract was developed to get coverage for the rapid launch of CET in as cost effective a manner as possible. Using Lee's company was the alternative that best met those requirements. However, for any service delivery process relying on contractual arrangements with a third party ... I'm going to paraphrase a Prussian military strategist ... 'No plan survives contact with reality.' In other words, expect to need to revisit the agreement and the process as more experience comes in because no matter how much you test it, you will still have some surprises. That is normal and I'm sure in this case, together we can improve the availability of CET."

That opened up a long dialogue. Whether people were following my lead, or didn't believe that throwing people under the bus was productive, no matter how good it might have made them feel, it became a great session ... probably one of the most positive meetings I had been at with leadership in a long time. Preston and Jessica were especially positive ... perhaps because they didn't get embarrassed in front of Jonah.

The meeting ran over time and to my great pleasure, no one ... especially leadership ... left early. We didn't come up with any solutions, but that was not the objective. The meeting did what it was supposed to do. It got everyone on the same page. Everyone now understood, not only did we have to manage availability, but with a little bit more help from Lee's company, we could.

I'd waited until everyone was gone before starting to pack up. It felt really good to have a successful meeting with an audience like that. I was almost ready to go when Jessica walked in and asked, "Do you have a minute, Chris"?

"Sure," I said. "Should we meet in your office? I'm almost done here."

"That won't be necessary," she said as she closed the door. "This won't take long."

Jessica sat down as I finished packing up.

"I want to commend you for the way you conducted the meeting today. Running a meeting with a vendor present is always difficult and when you put an unhappy CEO into the mix, things become much more challenging. I really appreciate the way you kept everyone focused on the issues and not letting them drift off into recriminations and finger pointing."

She wasn't going to say it, but I knew this was a thank you for not throwing her under the bus.

"You showed more judgment and maturity than I was expecting and it bears further watching. Keep performing like that and rewards will come ... I promise you."

"Thank you. I really appreciate the feedback ... especially positive feedback," I said. Now it was another "What would Sean do"? moment.

"I do have something I uncovered during my research that you should be aware of, about our relationship with Lee's company. It was not appropriate to bring it up during the meeting, but I am concerned about it from an ethical standpoint."

"Yes ..." All of her attention was focused on me.

"It appears that one of our company's employees not only had contact with members of Lee's company, but may have provided them with material information about our infrastructure environments, CET and our plans, before any official contact was made, or any non-disclosure documents signed. These contacts were outside the channels set up to evaluate Cloud vendors and would have given Lee's company a potentially unfair advantage over the others."

"Chris, I know you used to work for Lee, and it is obvious there is still some conflict between the two of you, but are you sure this is strictly factual and not some kind of personal vendetta? These are very serious charges. Any employee of the company who engaged in such disloyal and unethical behavior would be terminated immediately. It would not matter who it was. So I ask you in all seriousness ... are you positive"?

"I promised I would not reveal the source because of their concerns about being terminated, but they gave me enough information for me to confirm it from other sources. There is no doubt in my mind."

Jessica pulled out a notepad and said, "Okay. Give me the specifics. I just hope you are being factual about this."

I began describing the facts I'd uncovered about what Keshav had done, and when and how I knew it was true. As Jessica wrote, a thought came into my mind. I didn't have a lot of facts about Sean. It was mostly suspicions. Sean was such a positive force at the company.

Should I share my concerns, or just let it go?

Tips that would have helped Chris

1. It can be useful in solving an issue, and also be good for your career, to closely model your behavior after someone who does similar work and is successful at it. It is not as basic as simply mimicking them. You need to understand how they act and react, how much leeway they have with the audience because of past history or personal relationships, and how much is their personal style. Above all else, you must make your actions your own. If you do not, you will not appear authentic and may end up doing more damage than good.

2. Be authentic. When you try to be someone you are not, or act like someone else, it weakens your ability to sell your message to others, even if you are doing it to offset what you think is one of your weaknesses.

3. Be very careful and very confident when accusing other employees of offenses that would result in their termination. This is behavior that leads to your becoming exactly like the people who may have made your life difficult. Stay true to your values and who you are.

CHAPTER 14: THINGS ARE RARELY WHAT THEY SEEM

I sat in the coffee shop and stared at my freshly delivered glass of Vietnamese iced coffee, and watched the light and dark liquids intermix in a slow motion ballet. I'd bought it to celebrate the success of my presentation earlier this week. And that wasn't the only success. I'd been instrumental in getting Keshav exposed, and I had heard this morning that he had left the company. There were no details, but that was typical.

I was sorry about Sherm. If it hadn't been for his integrity and high ethical standards, I never would have known about Lee's plot to manipulate our company and enrich his company. I told myself that Sherm was being set up to be the fall-guy by Lee in the event anything went bad. There wasn't much I could have done to help him. He was going to get fired by Lee no matter what. I would have gone down the same way Sherm did if I hadn't been very lucky. I thought about reaching out to him to see if I could help him find a new job, or at least offer to act as a reference.

I wondered what happened with Sean, as like Keshav, he seemed to have fallen into the same toxic pool that was Lee. That was the one that hurt even more than Sherm. Sean had always been my friend ... at least I thought he was my friend. He always seemed to have my back. And his sense of right and wrong, as well as what was fair, had seemed impeccable. I couldn't figure out what had made him go bad.

What bothered me the most was that Lee remained untouched, as usual. And depending on the deal leadership set up with his company for help managing availability, he might even end up a little richer. Sometimes it felt like there was no justice.

I was reflecting on all that had happened when I heard a familiar voice call my name. It was Sherm. I turned around as he walked over to my table, drink in hand. I was glad to see him, and really wanted to know what he was going to do next. Perhaps if I could help him that would make up for what Lee had done to him. I waved him over and he sat down at my table.

"Sherm, it's good to see you. How are you doing"?

He nodded silently and took a sip from his steaming cup.

"I want you to know that I couldn't have done any of this without your guidance. You're the one who straightened me out about availability and capacity … about the way the two interact … how one is near term and the other is strategic. You really opened my eyes, and for that I am truly grateful. I just hope you're handling all that happened okay. Is there anything I can do to help you"?

He shook his head. "I'm doing great. It's been a really great week."

I looked at him quizzically. "You sound really upbeat given what Lee did to you and all. It's okay, I used to work for Lee. I know what it's like and how he treats people. At least you won't have to see him again."

Sherm looked puzzled. "Why won't I see him again? And why should I want to not see him again"?

"He just got you fired. You may be more forgiving than I am, but I can't imagine anyone wanting to hang around with someone who just had them terminated. It's okay to not like someone when they do those kinds of things to you."

"And what do you think I've done to my friend Sherman"?

I looked up and there stood Lee. "Sherman and I planned to meet here to have a cup of coffee. He said you introduced him to this place and he thought it was great, so I agreed to try it. Finding you here is an added bonus." Lee sat down and placed a cup of Turkish coffee, medium sweet, in front of him.

I sat back in the chair. My confusion must have been apparent.

Sherm turned to Lee and said, "You lost. Pay up."

Lee reached inside his suit jacket and pulled out a crocodile skin Ganzo wallet. He thumbed it open and pulled out a $100 dollar bill ... fresh and crisp, without a wrinkle or stain in sight. "Okay, you won the bet, don't gloat, just take your money and go. I believe you have a plane to catch."

Sherm put the money in his wallet, stood up, and reached across the table to shake my hand.

"Thanks a lot Chris, you set me up to make a lot of money off this account," he said with a grin.

"With $100"? I asked.

Sherm laughed and said, "Hardly. But maybe Lee will explain it to you. I've got to get to our next client."

A moment later he was out the door and I was left staring at Lee.

"What's the matter, Chris"? said Lee with a wide grin. "You look very confused."

"Didn't you fire Sherm? You said he was no longer with us, that he had gone on to other challenges elsewhere. That's standard corporate speak for someone being fired. And he revealed your pre-contract secret contacts ... deals with Keshav, and much as I hate to say it, with Sean too. And those ethical violations got them fired, too."

"I'm hurt that you would think I did something unethical. I've always prided myself on being honest, transparent and working for the best interest of all parties involved," said Lee.

"Please ... don't forget that I had to work for you. Besides, Sherm confirmed what you'd done, and I saw you meeting with both Keshav and Sean to discuss it."

Lee shook his head. "I'm very impressed with Sherman's work. Not only did he guide you to the desired conclusions, but he also let you lead yourself there without any extra effort from him. I'm really glad I took him under my wing. He's proven himself very useful. With my coaching he will go far."

"What about him revealing your plans ... and educating us on what needed to be done"?

Lee laughed out loud ... in a casual, almost raucous way ... something I had never seen him do before. It was so casual ... so inconsistent with my view of him.

"We subcontracted our Cloud services from a much larger company – everything from capacity to support. Effectively we billed your company a market competitive rate, received payments, and gave a portion of that to our subcontractor. At the same time, our service arrangement with your company was very specific, and focused on what was the cheapest and easiest for us to supply – capacity and level one support. However, if your company decided it wanted something else, then those services could be added, but at a contractually pre-determined much higher rate. And of course a much larger commission check for me ... and Sherman."

"So you cheated my company on the contract? You set my leadership up to incur a lot of charges they didn't know about"? I said. "How is that right? Forget that, how is that legal"?

"Look, we gave your leadership what they asked for. Their ignorance of what was needed, or willingness to be led to a solution, was none of our concern. We were under no obligation to tell them they were missing an element necessary to mitigate their concerns. Our job was to give them what they asked for, at a price that made sense to them. We're not responsible for your leadership's belief that they knew all the important technical and process issues that needed to be addressed. Adding a single person to their evaluation team, such as Keshav or Sean, would have prevented all that. As it is, compensating for your leadership's hubris will mean a substantial increase in revenue for my company."

"No ... remember that Keshav and Sean were already working with you. That's why they're gone."

Lee shook his head. "Nonsense. For a moment, I thought you might have understood it all, but it's clear you're still missing the point. I did speak with Keshav before we signed the contract, but it had nothing to do with this deal. I was just trying to understand if he had been working with your leadership or not. Remember, we used to work together for a long time here. And he hates my guts almost as much as you do – doesn't care much for your leadership either. He just thinks his design doesn't need any support from outside resources like my company. It's not about your company or mine. It's about his ego."

"Then why did they fire him? He must have done something wrong, or they wouldn't have done that," I asked.

Lee shrugged his shoulders. "I don't know anything about his leaving. Perhaps someone falsely accused him of doing something wrong and despite his protests he was let go." He leaned across the table. "Know anyone who might have done that"? Lee sipped from his coffee and said, "And as far as Sean is concerned, I knew him before you got here. I have a nephew applying to the same college Sean went to and I wanted Sean to talk to him about the school. It had nothing to do with this contract."

Lee drained the last of his beverage and then covered the empty cup with his napkin. He stood up, carefully straightened his suit, and began to step away from the table. "I must be going. I have a plane to catch and I know I am late. Sherman thought I was crazy to cut the time so close, but to be honest, to see the look on your face made it all worthwhile."

"Aren't you afraid I'll tell my leadership what you just told me … let them know how …"

Lee grinned and cut me off. "Let them know what? My company did nothing unethical or illegal. In fact, your leadership freely signed the contract, even after I advised them in front of witnesses to conduct a technical review before signing on with my company. They insisted it wasn't necessary; that they had all the knowledge necessary."

"And if they decide to limit their work to only the base level capacity support? What if they don't sign up for any more? What if they take availability management elsewhere, or even bring it back in-house"?

Lee turned and headed for the door. "Then my company and I are no worse off than we were before. For us there is only upside to this situation. I think you've already seen what will happen with CET without strong attention to availability management. Perhaps you are right. Perhaps leadership would rather explain to the Board of Directors why the results for the fourth quarter, and the year, were complete failures due to their own narcissism? I think not. I know from experience that when confronted with a choice between revealing their own mortal weaknesses and spending more of the company's money, it's a very easy decision for them to protect themselves and their jobs."

I went back up to the counter and got a refill on my drink. I was about to walk back to the table when I felt a hand clamp onto my shoulder. I turned around and there was Sean.

"I thought I might find you here. I sent you a meeting invitation for tomorrow morning. After your presentation today, I've been assigned to work with you to map out how quickly we can build an availability management process for CET."

"You didn't get fired"? I stammered.

Sean laughed and said, "Not yet … at least not that I know of. I've been out helping my sister close the sale on her vacation cottage and get her stuff moved."

Quietly I asked, "Did you hear about Keshav getting fired"?

14: Things are Rarely what they Seem

Sean shook his head. "Boy are you misinformed. He quit. He was fed up and had been looking for a new job for months. I've been trying to talk him out of it, but I couldn't. That's why I stayed behind to talk with him after you left. I wanted to offer to be a reference for him. He may be eccentric, but he's the best Director of Development I know. It really hurts us to lose him."

I shook my head. "Get a cup of coffee and sit down. We have a lot to cover."

Tips that would have helped Chris

1. Things are often not what they seem. If you let them, people can misdirect and mislead you to suit their own ends. The one protection you have is to trust but verify. Assume good intent but don't jump to conclusions. Misdirection and misinformation are the basis for most magic tricks. While that can be entertaining, on your job it can have grave consequences.

2. You will rarely have full and complete information when you make decisions. Just make sure you have as much as you can prudently gather.

3. Be resilient. Remember that life will go on. Each project has its own challenges. Availability and capacity are especially difficult because they deal with intangibles. So celebrate a little more than usual when you successfully roll them out.

ITG RESOURCES

IT Governance Ltd sources, creates and delivers products and services to meet the real-world, evolving IT governance needs of today's organisations, directors, managers and practitioners.

The ITG website (*www.itgovernance.co.uk*) is the international one-stop-shop for corporate and IT governance information, advice, guidance, books, tools, training and consultancy. On the website you will find the following pages related to IT service management and the subject matter of this book:

www.itgovernance.co.uk/itsm.aspx

www.itgovernance.co.uk/iso20000.aspx

www.itgovernance.co.uk/itil.aspx

www.itgovernance.co.uk/cloud-computing.aspx.

Publishing Services

IT Governance Publishing (ITGP) is the world's leading IT-GRC publishing imprint that is wholly owned by IT Governance Ltd.

With books and tools covering all IT governance, risk and compliance frameworks, we are the publisher of choice for authors and distributors alike, producing unique and practical publications of the highest quality, in the latest formats available, which readers will find invaluable.

www.itgovernancepublishing.co.uk is the website dedicated to ITGP. Other titles published by ITGP that may be of interest include:

- The Daniel McLean ITSM Fiction Series

    www.itgovernance.co.uk/shop/p-1526.aspx

- The ITSM Thought Leadership Series

    www.itgovernance.co.uk/shop/p-1398.aspx

- ITIL Lifecycle Essentials

  www.itgovernance.co.uk/shop/p-1285.aspx.

We also offer a range of off-the-shelf *toolkits* that give comprehensive, customisable documents to help users create the specific documentation they need to properly implement a management system or standard. Written by experienced practitioners and based on the latest best practice, ITGP toolkits can save months of work for organisations working towards compliance with a given standard.

Toolkits that may be of interest include:

- ITSM, ITIL® & ISO/IEC 20000 Implementation Toolkit

  www.itgovernance.co.uk/shop/p-872.aspx

- IT Governance Control Framework Implementation Toolkit

  www.itgovernance.co.uk/shop/p-1305.aspx

- ISO/IEC 20000 Documentation Toolkit

  www.itgovernance.co.uk/shop/p-632.aspx.

Books and tools published by IT Governance Publishing (ITGP) are available from all business booksellers and the following websites:

www.itgovernance.eu   *www.itgovernanceusa.com*

www.itgovernance.in   *www.itgovernancesa.co.za*

www.itgovernance.asia.

Training Services

IT Governance offers an extensive portfolio of training courses designed to educate information security, IT governance, risk management and compliance professionals.

ISO/IEC 20000 is the first International Standard for IT service management and has been developed to reflect the best practice guidance contained within the ITIL framework. Our ISO20000 Foundation and Practitioner training courses are designed to provide delegates with a comprehensive introduction and guide to the implementation of an ISO20000 management system and an industry recognised qualification awarded by APMG International.

We also have a unique ITIL Foundation (2 Day) training course designed to provide delegates with the knowledge and skills required to pass the EXIN ITIL Foundation examination at the very first attempt.

Full details of all IT Governance training courses can be found at *www.itgovernance.co.uk/training.aspx*.

Professional Services and Consultancy

Our expert consultants can show you how to best apply the lessons of ITIL, COBIT and ISO/IEC 20000 so that you can make process improvements and eliminate any 'gaps'. We explain the ideal and purpose behind each framework and then help you to find the most appropriate solutions to create a stronger and more robust Service Management System (SMS). By drawing on our extensive experience of management systems to combine service management frameworks, you can support the goal of delivering quality services that benefit the business - efficiently, effectively and economically.

We can coach you in the most effective ways to conduct enterprise-wide assessments. With our support, you will learn to describe the often complex interrelationships between different processes, recognizing and taking account of the various maturity levels.

For more information about IT Governance Consultancy for IT service management, see *www.itgovernance.co.uk/itsm-itil-iso20000-consultancy.aspx*.

Newsletter

IT governance is one of the hottest topics in business today, not least because it is also the fastest moving.

You can stay up to date with the latest developments across the whole spectrum of IT governance subject matter, including; risk management, information security, ITIL and IT service management, project governance, compliance and so much more, by subscribing to ITG's core publications and topic alert emails.

Simply visit our subscription centre and select your preferences: *www.itgovernance.co.uk/newsletter.aspx*.

EU for product safety is Stephen Evans, The Mill Enterprise Hub, Stagreenan, Drogheda, Co. Louth, A92 CD3D, Ireland. (servicecentre@itgovernance.eu)

www.ingramcontent.com/pod-product-compliance
Lightning Source LLC
Chambersburg PA
CBHW071130050326
40690CB00008B/1411